THE CLEAR PATH TO
HUMAN DEVELOPMENT

Human Science in Scriptural Language

The Clear Path to Human Development:
Human Science in Scriptural Language

Published by Niyah Press

Niyah Press books may be purchased for educational, business, or sales promotional use.

For information, please write the author directly: sabilillah@aol.com

FIRST EDITION

ISBN: 978-1-945873-13-3

THE CLEAR PATH TO HUMAN DEVELOPMENT
Human Science in Scriptural Language

Imam Faheem Shuaibe

DETROIT, MICHIGAN

To my mother,

Hajjah Tennye Faye Luper-Johnson,
[Double Masters Degree],

May Allah's Mercy be upon her who modeled
moral excellence for me and
who instilled in me an undying love for education.

بِسْمِ اللَّهِ الرَّحْمَٰنِ الرَّحِيمِ

سُبْحَٰنَ ٱلَّذِىٓ أَسْرَىٰ بِعَبْدِهِۦ لَيْلًا مِّنَ ٱلْمَسْجِدِ ٱلْحَرَامِ إِلَى ٱلْمَسْجِدِ ٱلْأَقْصَا ٱلَّذِى بَٰرَكْنَا حَوْلَهُۥ لِنُرِيَهُۥ مِنْ ءَايَٰتِنَآ إِنَّهُۥ هُوَ ٱلسَّمِيعُ ٱلْبَصِيرُ ﴿١﴾

"Exalted is He who took His servant by night from al-Masjid al-Haram to al-Masjid al-Aqsa, whose surroundings We have blessed, to show him of Our signs. Indeed, He is the Hearing, the Seeing."

(Surah Al-Isra 17: 1)

Contents

Acknowledgements xi

Prologue: Bismillahir Rahmanir Rahim xiii

Introduction: "In the Beginning" 1

The Seven Levels of Ascension 11

    Level I: The Strong Development of the 5 Senses 13

    Level II: The Elaborated Functions of the 5 Senses 23

    Level III: Intuition: Acquisition of Concepts Extracted from Matter (Metaphysical Apprehension) 35

    Level IV: Mudghatan: The Birth of the Cognitive Capacity to Acquire and Comprehend Knowledge 47

    Level V: Izaaman: The Logic Tools for Digesting the Knowledge in Matter with a Potential for Error 57

    Level VI: Izaaman Lahman: Universal Logic for Particular Culture 67

    Level VII: Khalqaan Akhara: "The Standing Place of Abraham" and All That He Represents 75

    Level VIII: Prophet Muhammed Achieving The Destiny in This Life Through The Application Of The Isra Wa Mi'raj 91

About the Author: Imam Faheem Shuaibe 101

Endnotes 103

Acknowledgements

I WOULD LIKE to thank Dr. Ba'sim Zaki Adib, Phd (Bronx, New York) and Dr. Hameed El-Amin (Huntsville, Alabama and Detroit, Michigan) for their invaluable contributions to this book.

PROLOGUE

Bismillahir Rahmanir Rahim

"Reconcile your life again with the nature created by G-d and then you will find patterns for your thinking that will bring you to the great destination that God wants you to reach for your capacity and your potential inside of you."

"Education: A Sacred Matter,"
Imam W. D. Mohammed

THIS IS YOUR own personal map to the Promised Land. The Promised Land, for most people, means a temporal, earthly destiny promised to those who believe in G-d. For some, it is eternal life after physical death, the promised reward for believing in G-d. Whether that perception is correct or not, G-d knows best. However, Imam W. D. Mohammed, (ra), *[Rahimallahu Alaihi May Allah's Mercy be upon him]* has clarified that the Promised Land is in our lifetime, and it has much more to do with our personal development and evolution as individuals and as a collective body. He calls it "the promised human destiny."

The subject of this book addresses the pattern within our original human nature that, when brought out and understood, provides the map to the Promised Land.

One of the aspirations of this writing is to serve as a skeletal outline that, when fleshed out, will constitute everything necessary for an authentic education true to the nature, needs and destiny of any human being.

Beginning with Adam and ending with Abraham, this publication lays out the stages of development, from the simplest and most fundamental nature of the human being to the full expression of G-d given human cognitive capabilities. As explained in the book, the big picture is illuminated in the portion of the Prophet's Night Journey (*Isra Wa Mi'ra j* الإسراء) wherein he was elevated and met, stage by stage, eight prophets on seven different levels (Jesus and John were on the same level – Level II).

Inasmuch as the evolution described in this miraculous journey is a figurative expression of the human intellect growing from simple to complex, the elaboration of appropriate curriculum and content can follow and flow naturally in accordance with the nature and needs revealed by the meanings expressed on each level of the Prophet's (ﷺ) ascension. The details of this will be the subject of our next publication, G-d willing.

INTRODUCTION

"In the Beginning"

THE PRIMARY PURPOSE of this writing is to study and explore the Quranic story of Prophet Muhammed's (ﷺ) Night Journey as it is mirrored in Surah Al-Mu'minuun 23:12–23:14) through the lens of Imam W. D. Mohammed's (ra) language and the consensus in contemporary cognitive developmental sciences.

From a biological and evolutionary perspective, we begin with the human's beginning: the functioning of the newborn human brain. The magnificence of the brain is alluded to in verse 23:14, where it is referred to as "another creature."

There are seven cognitive levels for the developing brain and neurology. Under natural circumstances, they develop fully in a human being from 0–17 years of age. Verses 23:12–23:14 reveal this development in very basic and general terms. When using Imam Mohammed's methodology to study the Prophet's Night Journey (*Isra' Wa Mi'raj*), we can uncover its deeper meaning and representation. His physical ascension symbolizes every human's spiritual journey on the Clear Path to Human Development through the Science in Scriptural Language.

THE CLEAR PATH TO HUMAN DEVELOPMENT: HUMAN SCIENCE IN SCRIPTURAL LANGUAGE

Our objective is to utilize very important keys that have been given to us and the world by Imam W. D. Mohammed (ra). These keys are tools that enable us, and anyone who qualifies to use them properly, to see the network of connections that bring enlightenment, encouragement and empowerment in any domain of knowledge. The structure of reality and the place of human beings in it are not often perceived or grasped by most humans. Never the less, Imam Mohammed's (ra) perspective enables us to see the abstract and actual roadmaps of human development and progress. The accurate discernment of how to travel those abstract yet concrete paths enables us to arrive at ever-increasing plateaus of achievement in any sphere of human endeavor.

Effectively, Imam Mohammed (ra) has given the world a legacy of master keys. This publication is based on a complete and thorough application of one of his conceptions—the science of scriptural language. The Imam summarized this concept in a national broadcast to the Muslim community in 1980:

> "Now, for all of these years that I have been working with the locks of secret knowledge, nothing has been as rewarding to me as knowing that actually exactness in Scripture, is abstract; and abstract in Scripture is exactness...
>
> Scripture will use figurative expressions, figurative speech and abstract symbols to address what is actual and what is scientific, what is very real...
>
> Figurative means concepts that have to be seen outside of the picture that they are given in.[1]

The present publication is predicated on this concept applied to the correlation of the Holy Qur'an, the hadith of Prophet Muhammed (ﷺ), the interpretative methodology of Imam W. D. Mohammed (ra), and the established science of human cognitive development.

Allah Knows Best.

THE HOLY QUR'AN SURAH AL-MU'MINUUN (THE BELIEVERS) 23:12–23:14

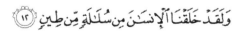

23: 12. Man We did create from a quintessence (of clay);

ثُمَّ جَعَلْنَٰهُ نُطْفَةً فِى قَرَارٍ مَّكِينٍ ۝ ١٣

23: 13. Then We placed him as (a drop of) sperm in a place of rest, firmly fixed;

ثُمَّ خَلَقْنَا ٱلنُّطْفَةَ عَلَقَةً فَخَلَقْنَا ٱلْعَلَقَةَ مُضْغَةً فَخَلَقْنَا ٱلْمُضْغَةَ عِظَٰمًا فَكَسَوْنَا ٱلْعِظَٰمَ لَحْمًا ثُمَّ أَنشَأْنَٰهُ خَلْقًا ءَاخَرَ فَتَبَارَكَ ٱللَّهُ أَحْسَنُ ٱلْخَٰلِقِينَ ۝ ١٤

23: 14. Then We made the sperm into a clot of congealed blood; then of that clot We made a (fetus) lump; then we made out of that lump bones and clothed the bones with flesh; then we developed out of it another creature. So blessed be Allah, the best to create!

THE REPORT OF THE PROPHET'S NIGHT JOURNEY

Narrated Malik bin Sasaa: The Prophet said, "While I was at the House in a state midway between sleep and wakefulness,... Al-Buraq, a white animal, smaller than a mule and bigger than a donkey was brought to me and I set out with Gabriel. When I reached the nearest heaven Gabriel said to the heaven gate-keeper, 'Open the gate.' The gatekeeper asked, 'Who is it?' He said, 'Gabriel.' The gate-keeper asked, 'Who is accompanying you?' Gabriel said, 'Muhammad.' The gate-keeper said, 'Has he been called?' Gabriel said, 'Yes.' Then it was said, 'He is welcomed. What a wonderful visit his is!' Then I met Adam and greeted him, and he said, 'You are welcomed O son and a Prophet.' Then we ascended to the second heaven. It was asked, 'Who is it?' Gabriel said, 'Gabriel.' It was said, 'Who is with you?' He said, 'Muhammad' It was asked, 'Has he been sent for?' He said, 'Yes.' It was said, 'He is welcomed. What a wonderful visit his is!" Then I met Jesus and Yahya (John) who said, 'You are welcomed, O brother and a Prophet.' Then we ascended to the third heaven. It was asked, 'Who is it?' Gabriel said, 'Gabriel.' It was asked, 'Who is with you?

Gabriel said, 'Muhammad.' It was asked, 'Has he been sent for?' 'Yes,' said Gabriel. 'He is welcomed. What a wonderful visit his is!' - (The Prophet added:). -There I met Joseph and greeted him, and he replied, 'You are welcomed, O brother and a Prophet!' Then we ascended to the 4th heaven and again the same questions and answers were exchanged as in the previous heavens. There I met Idris and greeted him. He said, 'You are welcomed O brother and Prophet.' Then we ascended to the 5th heaven and again the same questions and answers were exchanged as in previous heavens. There I met and greeted Aaron who said, 'You are welcomed O brother and a Prophet." Then we ascended to the 6th heaven and again the same questions and answers were exchanged as in the previous heavens. There I met and greeted Moses who said, 'You are welcomed O brother and a Prophet.' When I proceeded on, he started weeping and on being asked why he was weeping, he said, 'O Lord! Followers of this youth who was sent after me will enter Paradise in greater number than my followers.' Then we ascended to the seventh heaven and again the same questions and answers were exchanged as in the previous heavens. There I met and greeted Abraham who said, 'You are welcomed O son and a Prophet'" (Sahih Al-Bukhari 4:429).

THE FRAMEWORK FOR
"THE CLEAR PATH TO HUMAN DEVELOPMENT"

This chart represents an overview of the book. Each column shows the major themes, all of which are analogous in their meaning and repeated in each chapter and on each of the seven levels. The book explains in detail how the themes represent varied aspects of the same central concept.

Level	Sura Al-Mu'minuun 23: 12-14	The Isra Wa Mi'raj [الإسراء والمعراج] The Night Journey) and The Ascension of Prophet (ﷺ) Muhammed	Imam Mohammed's Tafsir on The Isra Wa Mi'raj [الإسراء والمعراج]2	Cognitive Science Dr. Lawrence Lowery Cognitive Development and Education
I	23: 12 (Sulalatim Min Teen) سلالة من ؛ طين "A quintessence of clay"	Adam (AS); ءادم	The potential in the 5 senses and in matter	The 5 senses
II	23: 12 ("Nutfah fi qarrarin makkin") نطفأة في قرار مكين ؛ "A sperm drop in a place of rest firmly fixed"	Jesus and John (AS); عيسى و يحيى	Spirit of the Body (5 senses) and in Matter expressing itself in positive and negative	Elaboration of the 5 senses3
III	23: 14 (Alaqatan): علقة؛ "Blood Adhering"	Joseph (AS); يوسف	Intuition	Acquisition of concepts within but above matter. (Abstract Metaphysical Apprehension)4
IV	23: 14 (Mudghatan):مضغة؛ "An embryonic lump"	Idris (AS); إدريس	Knowledge for the society; Universal Culture evolved from the benefits of the intuitive capacity in the human nature	"Classroom Consciousness," beginning to learn how to "think beyond 5-sense information." Comprehending "Multiple Class Membership." Recognizing that every quality of a thing represents its membership in the class of all other things that have that quality."

Level	Sura Al-Mu'minuun 23: 12-14	The Isra Wa Mi'raj [الإسراء والمعراج] (The Night Journey and The Ascension of Prophet Muhammed (ﷺ)	Imam Mohammed's Tafsir on The Isra Wa Mi'raj [الإسراء والمعراج]²	Cognitive Science Dr. Lawrence Lowery Cognitive Development and Education
V	23: 14 (Izaaman): عظما; "Bones"	Aaron (AS); هرون	Culture evolved logic; Tools for digesting the knowledge in matter: The potential for error.	Both Moses and Aaron are to be understood through their "relationship" in the Plan of Allah. So *"Perceiving relationships"* is a prime feature of the Aaron Stage. At this stage "abstracts relationships" between things are comprehended and used concretely.
VI	23: 14 (Al-Izaama Lahman); العظم لحما; "Clothed the bones with flesh"	Moses (AS); موسى	Classic education from the logic of an innocent Culture; Institutionalizing corrected Education after Error;	Combinatorial reasoning. Selecting organizing and reorganizing things or ideas according to one's purpose.⁵
VII	23: 14 (Khalqaan Akhara): خلقا ءاخر; "Another Creature"	Abraham (AS): إبرهيم	Our second father Abraham is the level showing the growth pattern for the intellect in its interaction with material world.⁶ Knowledge that preserves what is universal and keeps it from going astray; He is the universal teacher.	Able to develop a framework based on a logical rationale about relationships among objects or ideas in the framework, while at the same time realizing that the arrangement is one of many possible ones that eventually may be changed based on fresh insights.⁷

How the Book is Organized

Every major section of the framework (Levels I–VII) is comprised of 5 parts.

1. Quranic references for the particular level of the *Isra Wa Mi'raj* [الإسرء والمعراج]

2. The hadith for the particular level of the *Isra Wa Mi'raj* [الإسرء والمعراج]

3. Imam Mohammed's (ra) commentary on the prophetic figure for each level of the *Isra Wa Mi'raj* [الإسرء والمعراج]

4. The Quranic significance for the particular level of the *Isra Wa Mi'raj* [الإسرء والمعراج] derived, by the author, from The Holy Qur'an, Chapter 23:12-14

5. The Cognitive Science of Human Development, shown either as direct quotes or from the implications. For this component, I principally draw from Dr. Lawrence F. Lowery's publication *Thinking and Learning: Matching Developmental Stage with Curriculum.* (I chose this material not as a "stamp of approval" to what Allah and the Prophet have revealed or what Imam Mohammed has given us as *tafsir* on those revelations, but as a representation of the present consensus in the brain science community. It is a secular and scientific confirmation of what Allah has revealed. I also include it because Imam Mohammed says, "True science is the correct interpretation of the material creation." So, since the brain science community has come to conclusions that concur with what Allah and the Prophet have revealed, it can be pointed to in that regard as evidence of the truth that can be derived from the material creation, yet another confirmation of what Allah has revealed.) Each chapter ends with a summary that captures the human cognitive capacity and capability born on that level.

IT ALL BEGINS (AND ENDS) WITH ADAM

There is an overarching frame of reference that serves as the background, or perhaps the "code," needed to interpret the Qur'an and the hadith correctly as a guide to human development. It begins by accepting that the story of humanity, of every human to grace this earth, is explained and codified in the story of our first prophet, Adam (as)—the original human nature. As we explore "what happened to Adam," we invariably uncover what is happening with ourselves.

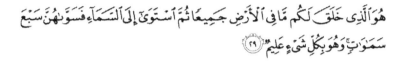

2: 29. "It is He who hath created for you all things that are on earth; Moreover, His design comprehended the heavens, for He gave order and perfection to the seven firmaments; and of all things He hath perfect knowledge." (Yusuf Ali translation)[8]

When we look at this verse through Imam Mohammed's lens of the science in scriptural language, we see what the revelation is revealing. We see that the first part of the verse, "It is He who hath created for you all things that are on earth," refers to how Allah has filled the earth with everything we need to fulfil our destiny and potential. The second part of the verse, which speaks of the seven firmaments, suggests that sacred human potential is fully realized by the full establishment of all seven stages.

This way of reading and this methodology is particularly affirmed because it leads directly to Surah Al-Araf.[9]

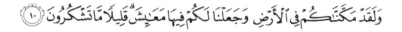

7: 10. "It is We who have established you in the earth and provided you therein with means for the fulfillment of your life: small are the thanks that ye give!"

This verse explains that Allah has placed your soul and its potential in your body, and that is everything you need to fulfill your life. More significant is that this reading leads us to verse 7:10, which is also the heading of the entire story of Adam, his wife and Iblis (7:11-27). Verse 7:11 begins with a confirmation of the body connection when Allah says, "It is We who created you and gave you shape." Then the story follows.

Through Imam Mohammed's methodology, this verse is brought into our view for no other reason than first "correlating the earth to the body" in verse 2:29. Read in this way, the understanding that 2:29 leads us to is, Allah has placed within the human being all that is necessary to fulfill his life on earth.

The phrase "Small are the thanks that ye give," which is found in verse 7:10 and other places, points to the grand favor G-d has bestowed upon human beings as an authority here on earth with the potential to achieve full life fulfilment. This potential comes in the form of the five senses through which we experience and affect the world. This connection will be clarified when we address the Level I explanation of Adam, *insha'Allah*.

In a fashion similar to verse 7:10, verse 2:29 is the heading, the preface, the frame and the foreword of the verses that follows. The entire story of Adam, his wife and Iblis from verses 2:30-2:38 is a *"figurative expression"* revealing the true, exact, sacred and scientific beginning of the human being as conceived and created by Allah.

Imam Mohammed (ra) says, "So don't just think Adam is something that happened in the beginning of creation. He is the depiction of something that continues in the life of mankind."[10]

He says also, "The story of Adam is the story of how G-d created the first person and that's the story of how G-d created every person."[11]

The Seven Levels
of Ascension

LEVEL I:

The Strong Development of the 5 Senses

QURANIC REFERENCES FOR LEVEL I

$$\text{ﭐﭑﭒﭓﭔﭕﭖﭗﭘﭙﭚﭛﭜﭝﭞﭟﭠﭡﭢﭣﭤﭥﭦ}$$

الَّذِىٓ أَحْسَنَ كُلَّ شَىْءٍ خَلَقَهُۥ ۖ وَبَدَأَ خَلْقَ ٱلْإِنسَـٰنِ مِن طِينٍ ۝

ثُمَّ جَعَلَ نَسْلَهُۥ مِن سُلَـٰلَةٍ مِّن مَّآءٍ مَّهِينٍ ۝

32: 7-8. Who made most excellent everything which He created and began the creation of man from clay. And made his progeny from a quintessence of the nature of a fluid despised. [12]

وَهُوَ ٱلَّذِىٓ أَنشَأَ لَكُمُ ٱلسَّمْعَ وَٱلْأَبْصَـٰرَ وَٱلْأَفْـِٔدَةَ ۚ قَلِيلًا مَّا تَشْكُرُونَ ۝

23: 78. It is He Who has produced you with the gift of hearing, sight, feeling and understanding: little thanks it is ye give!

وَٱللَّهُ أَخْرَجَكُم مِّنۢ بُطُونِ أُمَّهَٰتِكُمْ لَا تَعْلَمُونَ شَيْـًٔا وَجَعَلَ لَكُمُ ٱلسَّمْعَ وَٱلْأَبْصَٰرَ وَٱلْأَفْـِٔدَةَ لَعَلَّكُمْ تَشْكُرُونَ ﴿٧٨﴾

16: 78. It is He Who brought you forth from the wombs of your mothers when ye knew nothing; and He gave you hearing and sight and intelligence and affections: that ye may give thanks (to Allah).

قُلْ هُوَ ٱلَّذِىٓ أَنشَأَكُمْ وَجَعَلَ لَكُمُ ٱلسَّمْعَ وَٱلْأَبْصَٰرَ وَٱلْأَفْـِٔدَةَ قَلِيلًا مَّا تَشْكُرُونَ ﴿٢٣﴾

67: 23. Say: "It is He Who has produced you growing and made for you the faculties of hearing, seeing, feeling, and understanding: little thanks it is ye give."

إِنَّا خَلَقْنَا ٱلْإِنسَٰنَ مِن نُّطْفَةٍ أَمْشَاجٍ نَّبْتَلِيهِ فَجَعَلْنَٰهُ سَمِيعًۢا بَصِيرًا ﴿٢﴾

76: 2. Verily We created Man from a drop of mingled sperm in order to try him: so We gave him (the gifts) of Hearing and Sight.

THE HADITH OF ADAM ON LEVEL I
OF THE *ISRA WA MI'RAJ*

((THEN JIBRIL TOOK my hand and ascended with me to the nearest heaven, when I reached the nearest heaven, Gabriel said to the gatekeeper of the heaven, 'Open (the gate).' The gatekeeper asked, 'Who is it?' Gabriel answered: 'Gabriel.' He asked, 'Is there anyone with you?' Gabriel replied, 'Yes, Muhammad is with me.' He asked, 'Has he been called?' Gabriel said, 'Yes.' So the gate was opened and we went over the nearest heaven and there we saw a man sitting with some people on his right and some on his left. When he looked towards his right, he laughed and when he looked toward his left he wept. Then he said, 'Welcome! O pious Prophet and pious son.' I asked Gabriel, 'Who is he?' He replied, 'He is Adam.'"[13]

According to the above hadith, Adam (as) was the first of the seven prophetic[14] figures Muhammad (ﷺ) met on his Night Journey (Holy Qur'an 17:1).

IMAM MOHAMMED (RA) ON ADAM ON LEVEL I OF THE *ISRA WA MI'RAJ*

"The nature for the whole of matter holding all the possibilities for development or ascension is in the matter G-d created. Adam represents that. So Adam is on the first level."[15]

"Adam is like the composite seed of the total worth of the human person, materially, spiritually socially, or any kind of way you can think that is expressive of the human nature; and its ascent or its revealing or unfolding of what is contained inherently in the soul. So Adam is like a total seed, the whole seed. Then the seed comes to life and when it comes to life, it expresses what's in that seed on the first level. That's the common man; that's Adam." [16]

THE QURANIC SIGNIFICANCE OF ADAM ON LEVEL I OF THE *ISRA WA MI'RAJ*

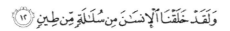

23: 12. By the certitude of my own reality[17] *– What follows this oath is more certain than your science. And that is that--We fashioned the human being (min) starting from a quintessence that began in (min) clay;*

MIN SULALATIM MIN TEEN (من سلالة من طين)

In the above verse, "a quintessence (of clay)" (*min sulalatim min teen*) means that the reality of the human being originated in an essence from an essence.

SULALATIM (سلالة)

According to Lane's *An Arabic-English Lexicon* (1893), the base stem *sulla*, from which we get *sulalatin*, carries the meaning of:

- Drawing forth gently from or of anything. [something drawn from something else]

- An extract of the thing hence the clear or pure part or the choice best or most excellent part of the thing.

- He drew the thing forth from another thing

- A young camel just born before it is known whether it is male or female.[18]

- Signifies a thing being connected with another thing.

A quintessence (of clay) (*sulalatim min teen*) is the unseen excellence of original human nature in its transitional state between non-existence (unseen) and existence (seen). Abu Huraira narrated: "They said: 'O Messenger of Allah! When was the Prophethood established for you?' He said: 'While Adam was between soul and body.'" So this *sulala* describes a nature that exists before it comes into the body. This perception is also supported by the following two verses:

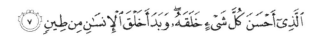

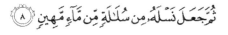

32: 7-8. Who made most excellent everything which He created and began the creation of man from clay. And made his progeny from a quintessence of the nature of a fluid despised."[19]

Between verse 7 and verse 8 above, you have a restatement of what is spoken of in 23:12. Verse 7 says, "We created man *min teen.*" Verse 8 says, "We made his progeny *min sulalatin.*" This book is also about learning how to read scriptural language and logic. Therefore, to state this directly, these two sections of the Qur'an are saying that man was created "*min sulalatim min teen.*"

However, the order and relationship brought out in Verse 8 *sulalatin* is from the concept of water. *Water* is a symbol of human nature and sensitivities. Also, "*sulalatin mim ma'in*" *is again* translated as *quintessence* because it is understood to be the "*essence of 5.*" *Sulalatim* is the seed of the five senses. Without the seed, no human existence, growth, or production is possible. Can you imagine a human being born without any of the five senses? How could they ever become conscious or produce anything?

ADAM REPRESENTS THE FIVE SENSES AND THE SEED OF HUMAN DEVELOPMENT

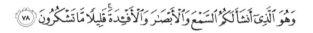

23: 78. It is He who has produced you with the gift of hearing, sight, feeling, and understanding: little thanks it is ye give!

The main verb in this verse, *ansha'a* أنشأ, connects us with the conclusion of our core verses (23:14 –*anshanaahu*). Yusuf Ali translates *ansha'a* as "created." However, in light of verse 71:17, which says, "Surely we caused the human being to grow from the earth like vegetation," a more fitting translation would be "produced," which carries the idea of vegetation—as in, the produce section of a grocery store. Furthermore, this verse supports the focus of our five senses as the first level of human development and the foundation of our distinction from all other creation.

If and when we understand the potency and power of this sacred foundation, the translation of *wa* as *harful qasm* (the letter of oath taking) is justified. The traditional opinion of *harful qasm* is that whatever Allah swears by has been elevated and honored. In this case, verse 23:12 points to how sacred the five senses are as the foundation for human destiny.

Other verses that emphasize the significance of the human senses are:

16: 78. It is He Who brought you forth from the wombs of your mothers when ye knew nothing; and He gave you hearing and sight and intelligence and affections: that ye may give thanks (to Allah).

This verse directly speaks to human evolution (*A-Kharajakum*) from brainlessness/knowing nothing (*laa ta'lamuuna shay'un*) to the development of the human intellect by virtue of the human senses (*As-sam-a' wa Ab-Saara wal af'ida*).

قُلْ هُوَ ٱلَّذِىٓ أَنشَأَكُمْ وَجَعَلَ لَكُمُ ٱلسَّمْعَ وَٱلْأَبْصَٰرَ وَٱلْأَفْئِدَةَ قَلِيلًا مَّا تَشْكُرُونَ ۝

67: 23. Say: "It is He who has produced you growing and made for you the faculties of hearing, seeing, feeling, and understanding: little thanks it is ye give."

This verse also connects us with the conclusion of our core verse (23:14 –anshanaahu). Ja'ala is a recurring term in these key verses as well. A very important connection should be made between the nature and the function of the developed human intellect and the following verse:

وَٱللَّهُ جَعَلَ لَكُم مِّنۢ بُيُوتِكُمْ سَكَنًا وَجَعَلَ لَكُم مِّن جُلُودِ ٱلْأَنْعَٰمِ بُيُوتًا تَسْتَخِفُّونَهَا
يَوْمَ ظَعْنِكُمْ وَيَوْمَ إِقَامَتِكُمْ وَمِنْ أَصْوَافِهَا وَأَوْبَارِهَا وَأَشْعَارِهَا أَثَٰثًا وَمَتَٰعًا إِلَىٰ
حِينٍ ﴿٨٠﴾

16: 80. *It is Allah who made your habitations homes of rest and quiet for you [1]; and made for you out of the skins of animals (tents for) dwellings which ye find so light (and handy) when ye travel and when ye stop (in your travels) [2]; and out of their wool and their soft fibers (between wool and hair) and their hair rich stuff and articles of convenience (to serve you) for a time.*

وَٱللَّهُ جَعَلَ لَكُم مِّمَّا خَلَقَ ظِلَٰلًا وَجَعَلَ لَكُم مِّنَ ٱلْجِبَالِ أَكْنَٰنًا
وَجَعَلَ لَكُمْ سَرَٰبِيلَ تَقِيكُمُ ٱلْحَرَّ وَسَرَٰبِيلَ تَقِيكُم بَأْسَكُمْ كَذَٰلِكَ يُتِمُّ
نِعْمَتَهُۥ عَلَيْكُمْ لَعَلَّكُمْ تُسْلِمُونَ ﴿٨١﴾

16: 81. *[3]; It is Allah who made out of the things He created some things to give you shade; of the hills He made some for your shelter [4]; He made you garments to protect you from heat [5]; and coats of mail to protect you from your (mutual) violence [6]; Thus does He complete his favors on you that ye may bow to His will (in Islam).*

The numbers I have inserted above represent six things man achieves physically. So why is it that Allah says He [Allah] did it *(Ja'ala)*? Each benefit mentioned is a transformation of circumstances that came about through the growth of the human intellectual capacity to solve problems brought on by the forces and demands of nature (environmental and human).

إِنَّا خَلَقْنَا ٱلْإِنسَٰنَ مِن نُّطْفَةٍ أَمْشَاجٍ نَّبْتَلِيهِ فَجَعَلْنَٰهُ سَمِيعًۢا بَصِيرًا ﴿٢﴾

76: 2. Verily We created Man from a drop of mingled sperm in order to try him: so We gave him (the gifts) of Hearing and Sight.

This verse connects our human senses with the next stage (Level II, *nutfatan*) in the progression. Allah says, "We tried him," (*Na'btalihi*[20]). This is the scriptural expression of the natural process by which Allah evolves man. Allah put the human being in an environment (human and material) wherein he must secure his own existence in the face of the forces and demands of nature. It reveals that Allah gave the human being the gift of the five senses so that he could pass the test.

Surah 55, Ar-Rahman, connects to the significance of the human senses by cataloguing the many blessings for human existence and then challenging humans to be grateful. It speaks to blessings past, present and future; from within and without[21] that either arise from or are experienced by the five senses.

THE IMMEASURABLE WORTH OF THE 5 SENSES IN SCIENCE AND RELIGION

"The brain processes incoming sensory data into and through the functional regions. The processing is done as the sensory data enter through the avenues of the five senses—all that we see, hear, feel, smell, and taste. The five senses are the brain's only way to obtain data about the 'outside' world."[22]

Imam Mohammed (ra) explains the greater meaning and symbolism of the five senses:

"See how powerful these five senses are to listen to you, to look at the sky and wonder about it, to hear the thunder and wonder, to smell the scents in the air and enjoy them and pursued these scents if I want to, to touch with my hand and know the difference between rough and smooth, between hot and cold etc.? So he gave me these five senses not just for my own body but

he gave me the five senses for my freedom and progress in this world."[23]

Imam Mohammed (ra) further explains that Adam is a personification of the nature for the whole of matter. Adam represents all the possibilities for the kind of development that is illustrated in the story of Prophet Muhammed's (ﷺ) ascension. Adam is the first expression of the potential in all of us, which is in matter (Holy Qur'an 30:30; *fitrah*). Consequently, Adam is on Level I in the report revealing our sacred destiny.

Both functionally and analogically, Adam signifies the five senses which are, as a matter of scientific fact, the foundation of human development. Other teachings of Al-Islam that have direct relationship to this reading are:

> *It was narrated that Ibn 'Umar (may Allah be pleased with him) said: The Messenger of Allah (peace and blessings of Allah be upon him) said: "Islam is built on five (pillars): bearing witness that there is no G-d except Allah and that Muhammad is the Messenger of Allah, establishing prayer, paying zakah, Hajj and fasting Ramadan."[24]*

*Ibn Abbas reported: The Messenger of Allah, (peace and blessings be upon him) said, "Take advantage of five before five: (1); your youth before your old age, (2); your health before your illness, (3); your riches before your poverty, (4); your free time before your work, (5); and your life before your death."*In Arabic grammar, there is the *ismul isharat*, demonstrative pronouns. These pronouns direct the reader to specific things (e.g., this, that, those, these). In Islamic teaching, there is what is called the *ishaaraat*. The *ishaaraat* are the concepts, ideas and meanings in a text or message that imply something without expressing it explicitly. Like demonstrative pronouns, they point to something else.

So, the importance of the five senses should not, must not, and cannot be divorced from the concept of five mentioned in both of the above *ahadith*. These saying of the Prophet (ﷺ) should be considered spiritually as they connect to the scientific reality of our human growth pattern. The idea that Al-Islam is built on five speaks to both our original nature and our religion because they are one and the same (see Surah Ar-Rum, 30:30).

The truth is that the structure of our life is also built on our five senses. The hadith that instructs us to "take advantage of five before five deprive you," as some translators say, also addresses the necessity of the proper use, development and elaboration of the five senses in order to have a fulfilling life.

Dr. Lowery and the cognitive development science community have elevated the significance of the stimulation of the five senses in the earliest possible stages of education.

The significance of this concept of five is acknowledged by the California Education Department, which has implemented the "First 5 California Children and Families Act." This act, known as First 5 California, established an educational program that seeks to support the brain development that occurs during a child's first five years of life. It focuses on the crucial five-year window of opportunity to engage young children in all of their senses to support optimal brain development. This shows that even a secular organization with no affiliation to Islam understands the importance of the five senses in the pursuit of human excellence.

First 5 California exists because research shows that many modern-day families miss the window of opportunity to support infant brain development. As a result, children have suffered. That research and resulting project prove the value of the Prophet's warning to "use five" to develop human life.

Level I Summary

Cognitive Development: The 5 Senses

Level I brings our focus to the five senses. It shows us the ultimate primacy and necessity of the five senses at the first level of human development because they serve as the foundation of our distinction from all other creation. They are the first vehicle of our advancement.

LEVEL II:
The Elaborated Functions of the 5 Senses

Quranic References for Level II

يَٰٓأَيُّهَا ٱلنَّاسُ ٱتَّقُوا۟ رَبَّكُمُ ٱلَّذِى خَلَقَكُم مِّن نَّفۡسٖ وَٰحِدَةٖ وَخَلَقَ مِنۡهَا زَوۡجَهَا وَبَثَّ مِنۡهُمَا رِجَالٗا كَثِيرٗا
وَنِسَآءٗۚ وَٱتَّقُوا۟ ٱللَّهَ ٱلَّذِى تَسَآءَلُونَ بِهِۦ وَٱلۡأَرۡحَامَۚ إِنَّ ٱللَّهَ كَانَ عَلَيۡكُمۡ رَقِيبٗا ﴿١﴾

4: 1. O mankind, be regardful of your Guardian Evolver, who formed you from one abstract entity holding the human nature of the male and the female and formed in the earth a bonded pair of a man and woman and from their human nature and their human forms produced many men and women. And be regardful of Allah, who you implore, and the wombs. Indeed, Allah is ever, over you, an Observer.

وَٱللَّهُ خَلَقَكُم مِّن تُرَابٖ ثُمَّ مِن نُّطۡفَةٖ ثُمَّ جَعَلَكُمۡ أَزۡوَٰجٗا

35: 11. And Allah formed all of you from the original essence, from a form holding the potential for both men and women then we produced you as a living pair.

وَإِذِ اسْتَسْقَىٰ مُوسَىٰ لِقَوْمِهِ فَقُلْنَا اضْرِب بِّعَصَاكَ الْحَجَرَ فَانفَجَرَتْ مِنْهُ اثْنَتَا عَشْرَةَ عَيْنًا قَدْ عَلِمَ كُلُّ أُنَاسٍ مَّشْرَبَهُمْ كُلُوا وَاشْرَبُوا مِن رِّزْقِ اللَّهِ وَلَا تَعْثَوْا فِي الْأَرْضِ مُفْسِدِينَ ۝

مِن نُّطْفَةٍ إِذَا تُمْنَىٰ ۝

53:45-46. "And that He creates the two mates - the male and female –From nutfah (male and female discharges) when it is emitted;

The Hadith of Isa/Jesus and Yahya/John on Level II *of the Isra Wa Mi'raj*

((THEN WE ASCENDED to the second heaven. It was asked, 'Who is it?' Gabriel said, 'Gabriel.' It was said, 'Who is with you?' He said, 'Muhammad' It was asked, 'Has he been sent for?' He said, 'Yes.' It was said, 'He is welcomed. What a wonderful visit his is!" Then I met Jesus and Yahya (John) who said, 'You are welcomed, O brother and a Prophet.'[25]

Imam Mohammed (ra) on Isa/Jesus and Yahya/John on Level II *of the Isra Wa Mi'raj*

"In the second level or plane is Christ Jesus and John representing the spirit in that matter, one representing the matter that holds the whole thing because after all, all of these seven evolved out of Adam, the potential was in the man that G-d made; the material that He made. So the second level represents the spirit in the matter and the spirit expresses itself in mainly two descriptions, one is positive the other is negative. Jesus (positive) and John (negative) (Peace be upon the Prophets). Jesus came to affirm and John came to denounce, but both are the same spirit. In man's spiritual body is the need to affirm and the need to reject or denounce. That's why they are on the same plane. Not because they're equal in their contribution but because they're equal in their nature, they're the same nature."[26]

THE QURANIC SIGNIFICANCE FOR JESUS AND JOHN ON LEVEL II OF THE *ISRA WA MI'RAJ*

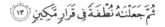

23: 13. *"Then We placed it as a binary fluid in a place of rest, firmly fixed;"*

The fullest explanation of Level II calls for an inclusive elaboration of not just the noun *"nutfatan,"* but also the prepositional phrase *"fi qararrim makeen."* The balance of this chapter is designed to accomplish that, *bi-idzini'Allah* (with Allah's permission).

NUTFATAN نطفة

The terms *thumma* and *Ja'ala* underscore that everything occurs in a repetitive sequence.[27] The *Ja'alnahu Nutfatan*جعلنه نطفة " expresses duality. The *hu*, which translates to "he" or "it," implies masculine form and is the direct object of *nutfatan*. The ending *ta al-marbuta* implies feminine form and is the second object.

One popular understanding of original creation is, "First came Adam (ﷺ) and then came Eve(ﷺ) ." However, that is not the Islamic picture. Another, more accurate, reading is that both male and female, as one unit, are Allah's intention in this process. We get the same picture when we apply this to Surah 4:1:

يَـٰٓأَيُّهَا ٱلنَّاسُ ٱتَّقُواْ رَبَّكُمُ ٱلَّذِى خَلَقَكُم مِّن نَّفْسٍ وَٰحِدَةٍ وَخَلَقَ مِنْهَا زَوْجَهَا وَبَثَّ مِنْهُمَا رِجَالًا كَثِيرًا وَنِسَآءً ۚ وَٱتَّقُواْ ٱللَّهَ ٱلَّذِى تَسَآءَلُونَ بِهِۦ وَٱلْأَرْحَامَ ۚ إِنَّ ٱللَّهَ كَانَ عَلَيْكُمْ رَقِيبًا ﴿١﴾

4: 1. O mankind, be regardful of your Guardian Evolver, who formed you from one abstract entity holding the human nature of the male and the female and formed in the earth a bonded pair of a man and woman and from their human nature and their human forms produced many men and women. And be regardful of Allah, who you implore, and the wombs. Indeed, Allah is ever, over you, an Observer.

The (نفس واحدة) *nafsun wahidatun* is the unit holding the nature and potential for both the male and the female, virtually and abstractly. Then (منها زوجها) *minha zowjaha* ("from it its mate") is likewise the new unit that is formed by the pairing of the biological male and biological female in procreation. As a pair, both (نفس واحدة) and (زوجها) represent what was/is potentially, virtually, abstractly in *nafsun wahidatun*. They are a "pair of pairs," one virtual (نفس واحدة) and the other actual (زوجها).

We see this expressed directly in Surah Fatir 35:11:

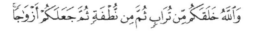

35: 11. "And Allah formed all of you from the original essence, from a form holding the potential for both men and women then we produced you as a living pair."

Allah addresses the same sequence in verses 23:13 and 35:11 with different elements. In 35:11, the verb describing Allah's act is *khalaqa* and the object of his act is *kum* ("you," plural; meaning all human beings). Therefore, verse 23:12 could be understood to mean, "I formed you all, originally, from dust (*min turabin)*" which equates to "*min sulalatim*/from an essence."

In both verses, "dust" and "essence" are followed by *nutfatan*, which is then made into "pair/s." Sequentially, there is first the created form from the essence, within which is an un-manifested duality, then *thumma ja'alakum azwajan*, which translates as, "He makes that created unit into pair/s (two)."

The *nutfatan* (the potential of both male and female) is from the *turaban* (original essence) and the *azwajan* (actual pair of man and woman) is from the *nutfatan*.

In the 65th verse of the 6th chapter of the Qur'an, Allah says, *"See how we explain the same thing in a variety of forms in order that you may gain understanding in religion."* In the following chart, there are three sections of verses that make the same point regarding "nutfah," but in different ways. It is established in Al-Islam that the best interpreter of the Qur'an is the Qur'an. But the help of Allah is indispensable to that aspiration.

The expressions in 35:11 and 4:1 are mirror images of each other. Read together with 23:12–23:14, they reveal important details about our sacred human reality and how it develops.

These verses show the creative process of the origin of the nature of males and females and how that nature is formed into the biological pair of a man and a woman.

On the first order, 23:12–23:14 of the Holy Qur'an gives the detail for the biological human being in the womb. It is also a sign of the graduations for the seven cognitive stages for all human beings.

All three of these verses give more explanation about the duality of male and female.

In verse 35:11, the three key terms in the verse are *"turaban," "nutfatan," and "azwajin."* They describe a transformation from dust to masculine and feminine potential (abstract and virtual) to the biological pair of male and female (concrete and actual).

Likewise, in verse 4:1, the three key terms in the verse are *"nafsin wahidatin," "khalaqa minha,"* and *"zowjaha."* When we compare these verses, we see that the end products are the same: "A pair of a male and a female," *"azwajin"* and *"zowjaha."* Verse 35:11 is direct in its statement, *"Khalaqakum min turabin,"* and 4:1 starts in the same way, *"Khalaqakum min nafsin wahidatin."* In the similarity and the difference, there is guidance. It is the similarity and the difference in the statements that illuminate the equation of *"turabin"* with *"nafsin wahidatin."* There's a duality that comes from *"turabin"* that is *"nutfatan,"* and from *"nutfatan"* comes *"azwajin."* There is also a duality that comes out of *"nafsin wahidatin.* That is, *"zowjaha"* after *"khalaqa minha."*

So, the logic of the equation of these two verses is this: Since their beginning is equational and their ending is equational, their middle must also be equational.

Nutfatan is "masculine and feminine potential in transition," and *khalaqa minha* is also "the intervening process of transitioning from an abstract pair into an actual pair." It is the dynamic interaction of natures of the masculine and feminine that give us the actual male and the actual female.

As obvious as this may sound, there is far more to it when you take that truth back into the verse, especially 4:1. But, *Masha'Allah*, we can't elaborate on that here.

"Nutfatan" (35:11) and *"khalaqa minha"* (4:1) have a correlated meaning, and when we bring 23:12 into the model and pair *"nutfatan"* from that verse as the 2nd term in the equation, then that puts *"sulalatim min teen"* as the first term and *"alaqatan"* as the third term.

Therefore, *"sulalatim min teen"* is equal to *"turabin"* and *"nafsin wahidatin."* And since *"alaqatan"* is the fertilized egg, which is also the product of the mixed male and female *nutfah*, it is literally the same as *"azwajin"* and *"zowjaha."*

Quranic Guidance for the Growth Pattern from The Virtual to The Actual Male and Female			
[35:11]	Turaban تراب "Dust"	Nutfatan نطفة (masculine and feminine potential in transition)	Azwajin أزواجا (male and female pair)
[4:1]	Nafsun Wahidatun نفس واحدة is "The unit holding the nature of the male and the female"	Khalaqa minha خلق منها (The intervening process of transforming the virtual/potential/abstract pair into the actual pair)	Zowjaha زوجها (biological male and female pair)
[23:12]	Sulalatim Min Teen سلالة من طين ؛ "A quintessence of clay"	Nutfatan نطفة (masculine and feminine potential)	Alaqatan علقة (The fertilized egg is the product of the mixed male and female nutfah)

As we said above, it is the dynamic interaction of the natures of the masculine and feminine *(physically and socially)* that give us the actual male and the actual female.

I must repeat, though it is a part of another subject, a part of that dynamic interaction is described by *"alaqatan." "Alaqatan"* also alludes to the social affections and attachments between the male and female, which begin the movement of society toward civilization.

Allah most explicitly states this in Chapter 53:45–53:46.

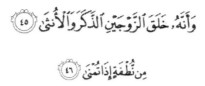

53: 45-46. "And that He creates the two mates - the male and female. *From nutfah (male and female discharges) when it is emitted.*"

Nutfatan[28] literally means "a drop of fluid." It also means mixed drops of the male and female sexual discharge. Prophet Muhammad spoke of the *nutfah* in the following hadith:

"Narrated by Imam Ahmad in his Musnad: A Jewish man passed by the Prophet (SAWS) while he was talking to his companions and the Quraish said, 'O thou Jew, this man alleges he is a Prophet.' The Jew said, 'I will ask him about a thing nobody knows unless he is a Prophet. O Muhammad! Of what is man created?' The Prophet (SAWS) said, 'O Jewish man, he is created of all, of a man's nutfah and of a woman's nutfah[29].'"

The "pure water" that is the *nutfah* relates also to the purity of the five senses. It is their purity that ensures their function for excellence in support of the progress toward human destiny. Imam W. D. Mohammed (ra) gives the following commentary:

"If your five senses won't bring you out of darkness, out of confusion, out of falsehood, then you have five senses that you think you're using, but you're not using them, your five senses are enslaved by falsehood...[30]

Muhammad the Prophet (peace be upon him) said, 'If a river or stream of water would pass by and you would wash in that water five times a day, would there be any impurities left?' His followers said no. ... He was telling them, in a wise way, 'Respect your five senses," because there is (i.e., they are like) a stream that comes and you wash in it five times and there are no impurities left in it after five times."[31]

The *nutfah* is the figurative and scriptural expression of the duality of the human subjectivity (feminine) and human objectivity (masculine) in connection with the elaborated function of the five senses in the material world. Scientifically, the *nutfah* is the transductive function of the five senses. It is the brain function that actually brings the external environment into our consciousness by transforming tactile, chemical and vibratory inputs into what we see, taste, touch, hear and smell. As human beings, we develop and grow by interpreting and responding (objectively and subjectively) to these inputs from our five senses.

In the progression of human cognitive development, Level II represents the elaborated functions of the five senses. These functions facilitate our human ability to interpret and label what we experience and respond appropriately (e.g., hard/soft, loud/quiet, white/black, sweet/sour, fragrance/odor, etc.).

John and Jesus are binary because they are on Level II and there are two of them. Only Jesus and John are binary in the Prophet's Night Journey. Transduce is a word that science uses to describe how our senses function to change vibrations from the environment into sounds in our brains, to change chemical molecules from the environment to smells and tastes in our brains, to change light from the environment into sight in our brains, and to change stimuli on our bodies into feeling in our brains. Each one of our five senses communicates to the brain the response to the input—the brain either likes or dislikes the sound, smell, taste, sight, or physical stimulus. In other words, it determines if we feel attracted or repulsed. On a spiritual level, Jesus and John represent this nature and function of the five senses.

Jesus and John on Level II Represent the Logical Pairing Capability

According to cognitive developmental science, the logical pairing capability becomes pronounced in the developing mind at the second of seven stages of cognitive development:

The second stage of cognitive development begins to unfold at about age three. Now, when the child thinks about objects and acts upon them, she produces pairings on the basis of size, shape, color, or other properties. Her rationale for each pairing is derived from the repertoire she has acquired through previous experiences. From this action, she establishes additional mental constructs about the world and how the objects and events in it are related. All her thinking is characterized by the ability to match two objects together on the basis of one common attribute, or to link two events on the basis of one relationship. This continues to be the dominant way in which she thinks and solves problems until about age six.[32]

In Imam Mohammed's commentary about this level, he states, "The spirit expresses itself in mainly two descriptions. One is positive, the other is negative.... In man's spiritual body is the need to affirm and the need to reject or denounce." This is the nature of the function of the five senses; to inform us of what is to be accepted or rejected.

Does it smell good or bad? Does it sound harmonious or discordant? Does it taste good or bad? Does it feel pleasant or unpleasant? Does it look beautiful or ugly? And, of course, we have moral and spiritual experiences in the same way.

More Qur'an on: Isa (Jesus) and Yahya (John) [pbut] on Level II Representing the Elaboration of the Five Senses

"Then we ascended to the second heaven. It was asked, 'Who is it?' Gabriel said, 'Gabriel.' It was said, 'Who is with you?' He said, 'Muhammad' It was asked, 'Has he been sent for?' He said, 'Yes.' It was said, 'He is welcomed. What a wonderful visit his is!" Then I met Jesus and Yahya (John[33]36) who said, 'You are welcomed, O brother and a Prophet.'[34]

This second heaven, where Jesus and John were seen, equates to the second level of human cognitive development (the elaboration of the five senses) which, like *nufatan*, also represents duality.

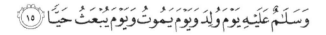

19: 15. So Peace on him the day he was born the day that he dies and the day that he will be raised up to life (again)! (Said with reference to "Yahya"/John)

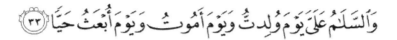

19: 33[35]. "So Peace is on me the day I was born the day that I die and the day that I shall be raised up to life (again)"! (Said with reference to Isa)

Essentially, both verses give the same conclusion regarding Jesus/Isa and John/Yahya. (They were also cousins.) However, there is a subtle and important message in the fact that the revelation addresses Yahya in the third person and Isa in the first person. This implies the duality of unconscious (Yahya is not speaking but is being spoken about) and conscious (Isa is speaking of and for himself). They are the five senses functioning on both levels: unconscious and conscious, subjective and objective.

It is significant that the Quran says of Yahya, "O Zakariya! Verily, We give you the glad tidings of a son, His name will be Yahya (John). We have given that name to none before" (19:7). This verse implies that Yahya is an attribute of the original human nature; His name essentially means life. He represents an unprecedented creation, human life, with nothing like it having come before it.

Zakariya had a "Mary moment[36]" by asking, "O my Lord! how shall I have a son when my wife is barren and I have grown quite decrepit from old age?" (19:8). These connections strengthen the dual nature reading, which ties Jesus and John together on the second level in the sacred plan of Allah for man's evolution to excellence.

Jesus and John, at the second level of man's development, are figurative expressions of the science in the transductive function of the five senses (i.e., the elaborated functions of the five senses). The five senses connect the human being to all of the information embodied within and projected from the nature of all matter. The five senses connect the inner life (subjectivity; activity beneath the surface) of the human being to the external world (objectivity; activity in the objects). The five senses conduct (draw, abstract, or extract; *sulalah*) the essences of the environment (particles, waves and vibrations; photons and chemical molecules; objectivity) into the human interior and transforms them as input for the brain to experience and understand the information to derive meaning from those sources (i.e., patterns, objects with their qualities, smells, tactile experience, sounds, tastes, etc.; subjectivity).

Fi Qararrin (في قرار)

Qarr- cool, calm, collected (colloquial meaning); contentment (vs. agitation and anxiety); acknowledgement, affirmation; rested stability; establishment; firmness; comfort; what formed the floor of Sulaiman's Palace (27:44; *Qawaarir*); clarity and purity (see *nutfa* definitions); set firmly (27: 40; *Musta-qirran*); permanence.

Ibn-Masoud (ra) narrated that the Prophet (ﷺ) said, "If a *nutfa [amshaj]* settles down in the womb[37] (*qararrim makeen*), the angel of wombs puts it in his hand's palm and says 'O Allah! Will it be created or not?' If Allah says it will not be created then it will not be a human being, and the womb will emit it as blood (miscarry), but if Allah says it will be created, the angel says, 'O Allah! Will it be a male or a female?[38] Happy or unhappy? How many years will it live? What will it leave behind? How will its living be? Where will it die?"[39]

Makeen (مكين)

Remember, the full phrase is: A place of rest, **firmly fixed**; (*nutfatan fi qararrim* **makeen**)

Makana - establishment, authority, place permanently; security; established position.

The essence of this state is the stability, establishment, firmness, rest and balance of man's original essence on this three-dimensional plane of time and space. The original human life is no longer between soul and body. With regard to man's cognitive development, this is also the stage wherein all five senses have become established and stabilized in their functions.

Peace is on us (Jesus and John; the pure function of the rested five senses) the day we were born, the day that we die, and the day that we shall be raised up to life (again).[40] Evidence of the resurrected senses is in every description of human life after death in paradise or hell.

As it relates to the function of the pure five senses as mediators of subjectivity and objectivity (transduction), they are not deluded in any way and there is no conflict between the two. The second level, ontologically and cosmologically speaking, is the stage where the excellence of the original human life is first manifested on earth, just as the zygote (the product of the female egg being fertilized by the male sperm) is established at that stage in the womb. Indeed, "a place of rest firmly fixed."

At this level in the progression, it's possible to perceive the simultaneous developments of soul, mind and body. Each of them now has the necessary foundation for their expression in this world. The mind has the body and the soul now has a mind and a body of its own.

Level II Summary

Cognitive Development: The Elaborated Operations of the Five Senses

Jesus and John represent the transductive function of the five senses. The five senses connect the human being to all of the information embodied within and projected from the nature of all matter. The five senses connect the inner life of the human being (subjective) to the external world (objective). They conduct the essences of the environment into the human interior and transform them into inputs that enable the brain to experience and understand the information and derive meaning from those sources.

LEVEL III:

Intuition: Acquisition of Concepts Extracted from Matter (Metaphysical Apprehension)

QURANIC REFERENCES FOR YUSUF ON LEVEL III OF THE *ISRA WA MI'RAJ*

وَلَقَدْ هَمَّتْ بِهِۦ وَهَمَّ بِهَا لَوْلَآ أَن رَّءَا بُرْهَٰنَ رَبِّهِۦ كَذَٰلِكَ لِنَصْرِفَ عَنْهُ ٱلسُّوٓءَ وَٱلْفَحْشَآءَ إِنَّهُۥ مِنْ عِبَادِنَا ٱلْمُخْلَصِينَ ﴿٢٤﴾

12: 24. And (with passion) did she desire him and he would have desired her but that he saw the evidence of his Lord: thus (did We order) that We might turn away from him (all) evil and shameful deeds: for he was one of Our servants sincere and purified.

وَلَقَدْ هَمَّتْ بِهِۦ وَهَمَّ بِهَا لَوْلَآ أَن رَّءَا بُرْهَٰنَ رَبِّهِۦ كَذَٰلِكَ لِنَصْرِفَ عَنْهُ ٱلسُّوٓءَ وَٱلْفَحْشَآءَ إِنَّهُۥ مِنْ عِبَادِنَا ٱلْمُخْلَصِينَ ﴿٢٤﴾

12: 53. "Nor do I absolve my own self (of blame): the (human soul) is certainly prone to evil unless my Lord do bestow His Mercy: but surely certainly my Lord is Oft-Forgiving Most Merciful."

يَـٰٓأَيُّهَا ٱلَّذِينَ ءَامَنُوا۟ مَا لَكُمْ إِذَا قِيلَ لَكُمُ ٱنفِرُوا۟ فِى سَبِيلِ ٱللَّهِ ٱثَّاقَلْتُمْ إِلَى ٱلْأَرْضِ أَرَضِيتُم بِٱلْحَيَوٰةِ ٱلدُّنْيَا مِنَ ٱلْأَخِرَةِ فَمَا مَتَٰعُ ٱلْحَيَوٰةِ ٱلدُّنْيَا فِى ٱلْأَخِرَةِ إِلَّا قَلِيلٌ ﴿٣٨﴾

9: 38 "O you who have believed, what is [the matter] with you that, when you are told to go forth in the cause of Allah, you adhere heavily to the earth? Are you satisfied with the life of this world rather than the Hereafter? But what is the enjoyment of worldly life compared to the Hereafter except a [very] little."

وَٱللَّهُ أَنۢبَتَكُم مِّنَ ٱلْأَرْضِ نَبَاتًا ﴿١٧﴾

"And Allah has caused you to grow from the earth a [progressive] growth."

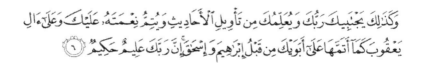

وَكَذَٰلِكَ يَجْتَبِيكَ رَبُّكَ وَيُعَلِّمُكَ مِن تَأْوِيلِ ٱلْأَحَادِيثِ وَيُتِمُّ نِعْمَتَهُ عَلَيْكَ وَعَلَىٰٓ ءَالِ يَعْقُوبَ كَمَآ أَتَمَّهَا عَلَىٰٓ أَبَوَيْكَ مِن قَبْلُ إِبْرَٰهِيمَ وَإِسْحَٰقَ إِنَّ رَبَّكَ عَلِيمٌ حَكِيمٌ ﴿٦﴾

12: 6. "Thus will thy Lord choose thee and teach thee the interpretation of stories (and events) and perfect His favor to thee and to the posterity of Jacob even as He perfected it to thy fathers Abraham and Isaac aforetime! For Allah is full of knowledge and wisdom."

The Hadith of Yusuf on Level III
of the *Isra Wa Mi'raj*

((THEN WE ASCENDED to the 3rd heaven and again the same questions and answers were exchanged as in previous heavens. There I met Joseph and greeted him, and he replied, 'You are welcomed, O brother and a Prophet!"[41]

Imam Mohammed (ra) on Yusuf on Level III
of the *Isra Wa Mi'raj*

"Yusuf (Joseph) is on the 3rd plane. And Yusuf (Joseph), in my understanding, represents the psyche. All of these are natural properties of human matter or creation that's all they are. So, Yusuf (Joseph) represents that and history bears it out. Why was he loved so much by the Ruler of Egypt? Because of his psychic powers."

"Then the third level [Yusuf/Joseph] is the great potential or the psyche of that [natural gross] body for arriving at knowledge without the use of the five senses or without the five senses being given the credit for that achievement or that success. It's not that the five senses are not used, but the five senses don't get the credit. That's intuitive knowledge, knowledge that we get by intuition."

"I'm talking about true intuition on the big scale, a universal picture. When you train to establish your life in the context of the world, then what is given if you're successful in having the intuitive spark come on, is direction for society in the world. That's the great Prophets, that's what they were given [in the Isra wa Mi'raj]."[42]

The Quranic Significance for Yusuf on Level III
of the *Isra Wa Mi'raj*

ثُمَّ خَلَقْنَا النُّطْفَةَ عَلَقَةً

23: 14 "Then We made the sperm into blood adhering (alaqatan).

Yusuf: A Young Mind

Alaqatin is a synonym for another Arabic term that means "occupations or such distractions that divert one from other things; occurrences that cause one to forget, neglect, or be unmindful." The following hadith is an example of this term.

Ibn Al-Atheer reported Muhammad (ﷺ) as saying:

> *"I have never tried to do what my people do except for two times. Every time Allah intervened and checked me from doing so and I never did that again. Once I told my fellow-shepherd to take care of my sheep when we were in the upper part of Makkah. I wanted to go down to Makkah and entertain myself as the young men did. I went down to the first house of Makkah where I heard music. I entered and asked: 'What is this?' Someone answered: 'It is a wedding party.' I sat down and listened but soon went into deep sleep. I was awakened by the heat of the sun. I went back to my fellow-shepherd and told him of what had happened to me. I have never tried it again."*

This is a state of youth before maturity, interpreted as a stage of realizing the most sacred potential in the human being. The various and progressive states are represented by the different prophets Prophet Muhammad (ﷺ) met during his journey. So, just as the reality of this state (*alaqatin*) is modeled in the actual childhood of Prophet Muhammad (ﷺ), it is also represented as Yusuf, the son of Yacub (Jacob), on Level III in the *Isra Wa Mi'raj*.

In both the Bible and the Holy Quran, we meet Yusuf (as) as a youth and learn of his suffering and evolving. Inherent excellence is also graphically depicted in his story in both books.[43]

Alaqatin also refers to a small garment or the first garment that is made for a boy. This has meaning for Yusuf's three garments: "one that was used to tell a lie on him" (12: 18), a lie that his father didn't believe; and "one that was torn from the back," the logic of which proved his innocence (12:26-28). The third garment was sent to blind Yacub at the climax of Yusuf's story (12:93-12:96).

Yusuf is a symbol for understanding the interpretation of things. Yusuf is on Level III in the *Isra Wa Mi'raj*, and he was also thrown in a dry well (12:15). It stands for a condition wherein the interpretation of things is not well[44] understood or that potential in its unrefined state. Yusuf is there, but he has to be drawn out (*alaqatin*). Yusuf is the apparatus (*alaqatin*) in us that brings out our natural capacity to understand the interpretation of things.[45] Yusuf represents the intuitive nature.

Zulaikah[46] and other women passionately desired him and wouldn't let it go, so much so that Yusuf preferred prison and wouldn't come out except on the condition that the women[47] were no longer a problem for him. The women are a sign of our immature attachments to things. Consequently, they typify those attachments that prevent the development of psychic power and intuition (Yusuf/Joseph). Even though the person may have some cognitive development, they have not developed their deeper potential to interpret phenomena with the benefit of intuition. That intuitive capability cannot come out under those conditions. Only after the person gives up their immature attachments will the intuitive capability manifest.

Cosmologically speaking, the essence of this stage is clinging, adhering, attaching, holding and hanging. At this stage, the original human life, on its upward journey to full maturity, begins to cling to, adhere to and attach to the physical life it has come to know on earth. It will remain in that clinging state for the rest of its three-dimensional existence until and unless it learns how to transcend the tendency to cling.

The story of Yusuf in the Qur'an is a crystal clear depiction of the challenge to the nascent sacred life at this stage. It speaks on the powerful grip of such natural clinging and how it requires the help of Allah to transcend it. Two events in Yusuf's life address this concept directly:

$$\text{وَلَقَدْ هَمَّتْ بِهِۦ وَهَمَّ بِهَا لَوْلَآ أَن رَّءَا بُرْهَٰنَ رَبِّهِۦ ۚ كَذَٰلِكَ لِنَصْرِفَ عَنْهُ ٱلسُّوٓءَ وَٱلْفَحْشَآءَ ۚ إِنَّهُۥ مِنْ عِبَادِنَا ٱلْمُخْلَصِينَ ﴿٢٤﴾}$$

12: 24. And (with passion) did she desire him and he would have desired her but that he saw the evidence of his Lord:

thus (did We order) that We might turn away from him (all) evil and shameful deeds: for he was one of Our servants sincere and purified.

وَلَقَدْ هَمَّتْ بِهِۦ وَهَمَّ بِهَا لَوْلَآ أَن رَّءَا بُرْهَٰنَ رَبِّهِۦ كَذَٰلِكَ لِنَصْرِفَ عَنْهُ ٱلسُّوٓءَ وَٱلْفَحْشَآءَ إِنَّهُۥ مِنْ عِبَادِنَا ٱلْمُخْلَصِينَ ﴿٢٤﴾

وَمَآ أُبَرِّئُ نَفْسِىٓ إِنَّ ٱلنَّفْسَ لَأَمَّارَةٌۢ بِٱلسُّوٓءِ إِلَّا مَا رَحِمَ رَبِّىٓ إِنَّ رَبِّى غَفُورٌ رَّحِيمٌ ﴿٥٣﴾

12: 53. "Nor do I absolve my own self (of blame): the (human soul) is certainly prone to evil unless my Lord do bestow His Mercy: but surely certainly my Lord is Oft-Forgiving Most Merciful."

We see from the above quotes that Yusuf was able to rise above his passion for her by what he knew from his Lord.[48] We have to do the same. The *nafsa la amarratu*[49] is "prone to evil unless my Lord do bestow His Mercy." No one can defeat the natural proclivity to err and follow their passions (i.e., their own jinn) without the mercy of Allah.

From the perspective of humanity at large, the failure to transcend is addressed in the Qur'an in the following verse:

يَٰٓأَيُّهَا ٱلَّذِينَ ءَامَنُواْ مَا لَكُمْ إِذَا قِيلَ لَكُمُ ٱنفِرُواْ فِى سَبِيلِ ٱللَّهِ ٱثَّاقَلْتُمْ إِلَى ٱلْأَرْضِ أَرَضِيتُم بِٱلْحَيَوٰةِ ٱلدُّنْيَا مِنَ ٱلْأَخِرَةِ فَمَا مَتَٰعُ ٱلْحَيَوٰةِ ٱلدُّنْيَا فِى ٱلْأَخِرَةِ إِلَّا قَلِيلٌ ﴿٣٨﴾

9: 38. "O you who have believed, what is [the matter] with you that, when you are told to go forth in the cause of Allah , you cling heavily to the earth? Are you satisfied with the life of this world

*rather than the Hereafter? But what is the enjoyment of worldly
life compared to the Hereafter except a [very] little."*

This is the existential tension in the life of every person from
the beginning to the end of life and development. Each person must
ponder, "How do I relate to my life in this world and to my hope for life
in the next?"

Growing Gradually from
the Earth like a Plant

Al-ghirass[50] *tabdalu bi-uluuq*: "The set or shoot that is planted
becomes changed by pullulating." It is a metaphorical phrase, meaning
what is planted becomes changed because it increases and rises when
it clings to the earth and germinates.

Imam Mohammed (ra) refers to this phenomenon when he
discusses the growth of human consciousness:

> *"God raises us up. He creates us in this earth.
> Our physical essences are of this creation, of
> this earth—in this physical universe. ...And God
> has already set the pattern of that growth, that
> progress, in the physical matter that we are from.*
>
> *...The physical matter has the pattern [like a seed with
> its plant inside of it, 91:7-10]. The pattern is in my physi-
> ology.... God has designed all of this! And it brings us up
> step by step (until) we become a part of a social order,
> living and interacting with each other."*

At this stage in the life process, the *fitrah*, the human life creation,
is at the point where its appetite is to express all of its inherent possibilities in this world. Its aim now is for the original destiny. At this
stage, it begins to change, increase and rise because of its attachment
to the material life. This is one of the significances of the following
verse in Surah Nuh.[51]

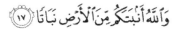

71: 17. "And Allah has caused you to grow from the earth a [progressive] growth."

With regard to man's cognitive development, since all five senses have matured and stabilized in their functions (Level I and Level II), they begin to attach the inner life to the outer life (transduction) and give matter its significance and attraction. Due to the nature of their very operation, the engagement of the five senses is both a blessing and a challenge because there is so much to see, taste, touch, hear and smell.

Cognitively speaking, this current stage must mature by overcoming the dominance of the five senses on its perceptions and judgment. This is the science that part of Yusuf's story is speaking of—freeing our thinking from the domination of the bodily senses. In cognitive science, this Level III is known as the pre-concrete operational stage.

Maturity (stabilization in the person) is required in order to come into the next stage: the concrete operational stage. In this stage, the person is able to use nascent, simple logic (i.e., a higher capacity of the mind) because they have begun to overcome the dominance of their senses on their perception (i.e., overcome cognitive clinging).

Yusuf III - to Idris IV

From Pre-Concrete Operational to Classroom Consciousness

The pre-concrete operational stage is one wherein the developing mind is still "five-sense dependent" for judgment. In the field of cognitive development, the concrete operational stage is called classroom consciousness. Of course, it is a natural fit for Idris, who will be addressed in the next section, Level IV. Classroom consciousness, in its primary stages, involves beginning to learn how to think beyond the five senses. In the secondary phases for older persons, it is the skill of not allowing our thinking and perception to be illogically or materially dominated.[52]

A child who is in the pre-concrete operational stage can be experimentally demonstrated to be at that stage. The one who conducts the demonstration can simply show the child two palm-sized balls of Play-Doh and ask if they are the same. This child will say yes because they see that they are the same size. Then the demonstrator can set the two balls on a table in front of the child and roll one out into the form of a snake or a rod. The demonstrator can then ask the child, "Which one has more?" The child will say the one that now looks like a snake or a rod has more. Why? Because that child is still five-sense dominated. He is looking at the fact that it is longer and, because of that, believes it is now more than the other.

A child that is beyond that stage of development can be asked the same question and will know they are still equal. However, the child may not be able to articulate how she knows that they're still the same. That simple logic exists in their own mind, which says, "The long snake is the same as the ball. Nothing was added to it and nothing was taken away from it, so they are still the same even though they have a different shape." That child has crossed the bridge from the pre-concrete operational stage to the concrete operational stage. She is no longer dominated by her senses. She has begun to use logic. This is the very beginning of logic: to learn that there is more to an object than what meets the eye.

Alaqatan – Yusuf and the Cognitive Capability of Interpretation

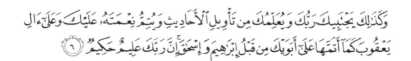

12: 6. "Thus will thy Lord choose thee and teach thee the interpretation of stories (and events) and perfect His favor to thee and to the posterity of Jacob even as He perfected it to thy fathers Abraham and Isaac aforetime! For Allah is full of knowledge and wisdom."

The primary ability that Yusuf is noted for is the interpretation of dreams. This refers scientifically to the birth of this ability in the young mind. At this stage, the human being "develops understandings that go beyond the properties inherent in the materials." Relative to our developing cognitive capacity, it is the beginning of our capability for abstraction (drawing out). It is also at such an early age that an evolving person is still subject to distraction by their senses.

Level III entails the capability of correlating and differentiating concrete things (abstracting, conceptualizing) on the basis of a simple rule applied to the attributes of the objects.

The chart below gives an illustration using a set of different types of leaves. When the Level III capacity is fully developed, the individual is able to look at the various characteristics of the leaves (or any other set of things) and by their ability to discern and distinguish characteristics of the whole (abstract, conceptualize), they are able to create and disassemble various groups based on a selected characteristic.

Stage 3
EXAMPLE OF WHAT LEARNERS DO

Given a set of objects, such as leaves, the student groups together or takes apart sets of objects based upon a single, consistent rationale. When the action is finished, sets of objects have a logic to their arrangement.

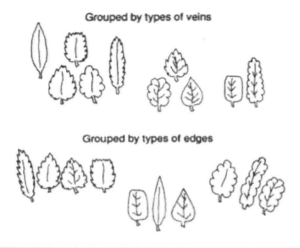

Grouped by types of veins

Grouped by types of edges

53

The *masdari* (root meaning) of *alaqatan* is, "all the apparatuses used for drawing water by means of the pulley." Level III, *alaqatan*, is the stage where natural brain development has assembled all of the apparatuses (embryonic capacity for logic) that will be used to draw out meaning from matter. It's the birth of the capability to read and interpret the signs in creation, human and material, but it's just beginning.

LEVEL III SUMMARY

COGNITIVE DEVELOPMENT: INTUITION- THE ACQUISITION OF CONCEPTS WITHIN AND ABOVE MATTER (METAPHYSICAL APPREHENSION)

Yusuf is a symbol for our ability to understand and interpret things. On Level III, he represents the cognitive apparatus (*alaqatin*) in us that is our natural capacity to understand the interpretation of things. Yusuf symbolizes our intuitive nature. Specifically, he represents the early stages of our natural intuitive capacities. Even though the person may have some cognitive development, they have not yet developed their deeper potential to interpret phenomena with the benefit of intuition. Only after the person gives up their immature attachments will the intuitive capability fully manifest.

LEVEL IV:

Mudghatan: The Birth of the Cognitive Capacity to Acquire and Comprehend Knowledge

QURANIC REFERENCES FOR IDRIS ON LEVEL IV OF THE *ISRA WA MI'RAJ*

39: 18.Those who listen to the Word and follow the best (meaning) in it: those are the ones whom Allah has guided, and those are the ones endued with understanding.

يَـٰٓأَيُّهَا ٱلنَّاسُ إِن كُنتُمۡ فِى رَيۡبٍ مِّنَ ٱلۡبَعۡثِ فَإِنَّا خَلَقۡنَٰكُم مِّن تُرَابٍ ثُمَّ مِن نُّطۡفَةٍ ثُمَّ مِنۡ عَلَقَةٍ ثُمَّ مِن مُّضۡغَةٍ مُّخَلَّقَةٍ وَغَيۡرِ مُخَلَّقَةٍ لِّنُبَيِّنَ لَكُمۡۚ وَنُقِرُّ فِى ٱلۡأَرۡحَامِ مَا نَشَآءُ إِلَىٰٓ أَجَلٍ مُّسَمًّى ثُمَّ نُخۡرِجُكُمۡ طِفۡلٗا ثُمَّ لِتَبۡلُغُوٓاْ أَشُدَّكُمۡۖ وَمِنكُم مَّن يُتَوَفَّىٰ وَمِنكُم مَّن يُرَدُّ إِلَىٰٓ أَرۡذَلِ ٱلۡعُمُرِ لِكَيۡلَا يَعۡلَمَ مِنۢ بَعۡدِ عِلۡمٖ شَيۡـًٔاۚ وَتَرَى ٱلۡأَرۡضَ هَامِدَةٗ فَإِذَآ أَنزَلۡنَا عَلَيۡهَا ٱلۡمَآءَ ٱهۡتَزَّتۡ وَرَبَتۡ وَأَنۢبَتَتۡ مِن كُلِّ زَوۡجِۭ بَهِيجٖ ۝

"O PEOPLE, IF YOU should be in doubt about the Resurrection, then [consider that] indeed, We created you from dust, then from a sperm-drop, then from a clinging clot, and then from a lump of flesh, formed and unformed - that We may show you. And We settle in the wombs whom We will for a specified term, then We bring you out as a child, and then [We develop you] that you may reach your [time of] maturity. And among you is he who is taken in [early] death, and among you is he who is returned to the most decrepit [old] age so that he knows, after [once having] knowledge, nothing. And you see the earth barren, but when We send down upon it rain, it quivers and swells and grows [something] of every beautiful kind."

THE HADITH OF IDRIS ON LEVEL IV
OF THE *ISRA WA MI'RAJ*

"Then we ascended to the 4th heaven and again the same questions and answers were exchanged as in the previous heavens. There I met Idris and greeted him. He said, 'You are welcomed, O brother and Prophet.'"[54]

Imam Mohammed (ra) on Idris on Level IV of the *Isra Wa Mi'raj*

> *"The fourth level is Idris and look how the language of Al-Islam helps us. Idris literally means study. It's taken from the root meaning study, lesson. Darasa means to study something; Idris means he is associated with lessons, study.*

So, Idris represents knowledge for the society. This is knowledge for the human society. This is not localized knowledge. All of this is talking about what is universal. So Idris is knowledge for the society and he is representing the universal culture of mankind. We have our local culture but we also have our universal culture. So he represents the cultures of mankind, isn't that how man has evolved?

So, we have that [psychic power/intuition] on the third level and then because of that, on the fourth level, it makes possible direction for ourselves in the world; knowledge. Culture comes as a result of the mind benefitting from intuitive knowledge. That's how it comes.[55]"

The Quranic Significance for Idris on Level IV of The *Isra Wa Mi'raj*

مُضْغَةً فَخَلَقْنَا ٱلْمُضْغَةَ عِظَٰمًا

23: 14. "...into a lump [of flesh], and We made [from] the lump, bones..."

Mudghatan (مضغة)

The methodology of Imam Mohammed (ra) incorporates the importance of the sound of words. Phonetics sometimes ties words together semantically and by interpretation.

"You know that language has those subtle hints and Allah said they believe that man was made from clay and Allah said "from sounding clay," potters' clay that makes a sound. It rings. So the wisdom there, the guidance there, I understand it to be, is that man has to have an ear for the sound of words. How they sound[56]*"*

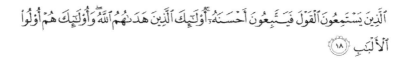

39: 18.Those who listen to the Word, and follow the best (meaning) in it: those are the ones whom Allah has guided, and those are the ones endued with understanding.

What is "Idris"?

Da (Daud) ra sa ("to bite firmly")[57] is phonetically tied to Idris. Even though the Arabic "d" in Idris is "dal," both terms belong to the same phonetic family called dentals. Dentals are speech sounds articulated with the tongue tip touching the back of the upper front teeth or immediately above them. The fact that both words are dentals and, at this level, are clearly connected with Level IV of the *Isra Wa Mi'raj* and that *mudghatan* is fourth in the progression (shown in 23:12–23:14) has great significance.

By definition, *mudghatan* means "what remains after chewing (mastication)." *Mudghatan* is tied to *darasa* "to bite firmly." *Darasa* is tied to Idris as Imam Mohammed (ra) states, "Idris literally means study…. Darasa means to study something." Furthermore, the word "*talib*," which is used for "student" also carries within it the meaning "appetite," which also involves teeth and chewing. Just some food for thought.

23: 14. "...into a lump [of flesh], and We made [from] the lump, bones..."

The Quran clearly states that the *mudghatan* is transformed into bone (*izaaman*[58]) and the bones are covered by flesh (muscles). This Quranic revelation is affirmed by modern embryology, which uses the word "somite." *Mudghatan* differentiates into:

A. Sclerotome from which the skeletal system is formed (Level V; Aaron; Logic)

B. Myotome from which the muscular system is formed. (Level VI; Moses: Corrected Education)

In embryology, the skeletal system precedes the muscular system. The bone, once formed, is then wrapped by flesh (muscle), as stated in 23:14. Physically and cognitively speaking, both these embryological facts mean that the *mudghatan* is the beginning of the *izaaman*/bone though not yet mature. Additionally, this cycle of repetitive indefiniteness to definiteness is the motif of each step in this section of verses 23:12–23:14.

Mudghatan is elaborated upon in Surah Al-Hajj 22:5.

يَٰٓأَيُّهَا ٱلنَّاسُ إِن كُنتُمْ فِى رَيْبٍ مِّنَ ٱلْبَعْثِ فَإِنَّا خَلَقْنَٰكُم مِّن تُرَابٍ ثُمَّ مِن نُّطْفَةٍ ثُمَّ مِنْ عَلَقَةٍ ثُمَّ مِن مُّضْغَةٍ مُّخَلَّقَةٍ وَغَيْرِ مُخَلَّقَةٍ لِّنُبَيِّنَ لَكُمْ وَنُقِرُّ فِى ٱلْأَرْحَامِ مَا نَشَآءُ إِلَىٰٓ أَجَلٍ مُّسَمًّى ثُمَّ نُخْرِجُكُمْ طِفْلًا ثُمَّ لِتَبْلُغُوٓا۟ أَشُدَّكُمْ وَمِنكُم مَّن يُتَوَفَّىٰ وَمِنكُم مَّن يُرَدُّ إِلَىٰٓ أَرْذَلِ ٱلْعُمُرِ لِكَيْلَا يَعْلَمَ مِنۢ بَعْدِ عِلْمٍ شَيْـًٔا وَتَرَى ٱلْأَرْضَ هَامِدَةً فَإِذَآ أَنزَلْنَا عَلَيْهَا ٱلْمَآءَ ٱهْتَزَّتْ وَرَبَتْ وَأَنۢبَتَتْ مِن كُلِّ زَوْجٍۭ بَهِيجٍ ٥

22: 5. "O People, if you should be in doubt about the Resurrection, then [consider that] indeed, We created you from dust, then from a sperm-drop, then from a clinging clot, and then from a lump of flesh, formed and unformed - that We may show you. And We settle in the wombs whom We will for a specified term, then We

51

bring you out as a child, and then [We develop you] that you may reach your [time of] maturity. And among you is he who is taken in [early] death, and among you is he who is returned to the most decrepit [old] age so that he knows, after [once having] knowledge, nothing. And you see the earth barren, but when We send down upon it rain, it quivers and swells and grows [something] of every beautiful kind."

Mudghatan is described as being "a lump of flesh, formed and unformed." Either way, it describes both the bone and the flesh at the stage. At the *mudghatan* stage, the bone (sclerotome) is formed and unformed and the flesh/muscle (myotome) is also formed and unformed. Though the skeletal system comes before teeth,[59] the *ayah*/sign is in the nature of what is being pointed to by the term *mudghatan* rather than the explicit and sequential relationship between baby teeth and the skeletal structure.

Mudghatan, by symbolic interpretation, belongs to the same semantic field as baby teeth. It points, figuratively, to baby teeth and how with baby teeth the child can begin to chew solid food. Those baby teeth are a sign of the nascent capacity for logic coming into concrete operation in the human being at the fourth level.[60]

THE COGNITIVE SKILL SET AT LEVEL IV

Establishment on Level IV gives the human being "the ability to recognize that every quality of a thing represents a membership in the class of all other things that have those qualities." A simple example is a shoe and a cup. Though they may seem completely different, they both belong to the class of things that can contain something.

This cognitive capability enables us to recognize that a thing can belong to more than one class at the same time based on the various qualities it possesses. Through this capability, we can conceptualize the intersection of ideas and understand the logic of the set that results.

The chart below illustrates how Level IV is about class membership, classification and how every attribute of anything constitutes a membership in the class of anything else that has those attributes. So, that same group of leaves can be reordered, grouped and reclassified on the basis of various attributes.

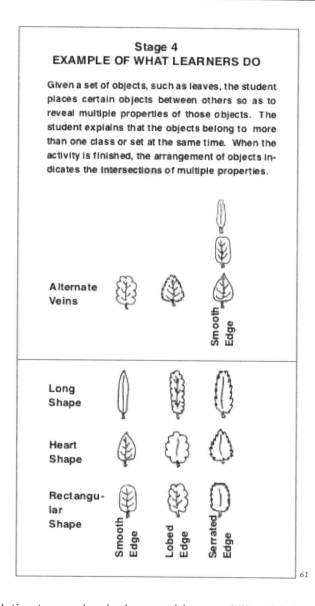

Stage 4
EXAMPLE OF WHAT LEARNERS DO

Given a set of objects, such as leaves, the student places certain objects between others so as to reveal multiple properties of those objects. The student explains that the objects belong to more than one class or set at the same time. When the activity is finished, the arrangement of objects indicates the intersections of multiple properties.

Relative to our developing cognitive capability, this level is the beginning of the concrete operational stage. The stage wherein the person is able to use nascent, simple logic. It's no mere coincidence that this stage is also known in the field of cognitive science as classroom consciousness (i.e., Idris).

Surah 22:5 is the only other distinct verse in which *mudghatan* is mentioned. Grammatically, *mudghatan* in that verse is called an ellipsis. An ellipsis is an end point that is understood not to be the actual end of a more complete series or thought.[62] In this case, the ellipsis relates to the complete development of the human being in the womb, as mentioned in 23:14. Therefore, the very language of Surah 22:5 rather poetically alludes to the significance of that feature in the movement of human development at the *mudghatan* stage.

Allah says He takes some things to full term and some He does not. As guidance, he says, "For example, take a look at the idea in the first part of this verse. It may seem, at first glance, that the thought has been aborted, but by that very sentence pattern, you should understand that it is also part of the explanation of the verse (*linubayyana lakum*)."

Surah 22:5 also points to the acquisition and loss of knowledge as a key feature of our cycle of human existence. *Mudghatan* is a stage in the development of cognitive capacity for the conscious acquisition and comprehension of knowledge.[63] At this stage, that capacity is partially formed and partially unformed, active but not yet stable and mature.

From a sacred evolutionary perspective, the essence of this state is the transition stage of the original human nature from unconscious to conscious[64] (partly formed and partly unformed).

If you interact with or watch a 3-5year old child, it would seem that they are wide awake, alive and conscious—but not so. It's very rare if ever that an adult has stream-of-conscious memories of their life at that age. The reason is that up to about 6 or 7 years old, the human being is in a hypnagogic state. The first 6 or 7 years represent the stage for taking impressions (like something chewed has taken impressions) and "downloading" from the environment whatever the five senses deliver (*alaqatan*). The child is like impressionable clay for the first 7 years of life. In fact, the English word "infant" is from the French word *infans*, which means "without speech." Figuratively, the human being is an infant until 7 years of age, when the ability to use the speech apparatus stabilizes and the child cannot only take impressions, but can also begin to give intelligible expressions. Yet as you listen, you will notice that their speech patterns are partially formed and partially unformed.

These facts of human anatomical and cognitive development are a virtual perfect fit for the next stage of the *Isra wa Mi'raj* and the next progressive development in our key verses (23:12–12:14) Aaron/Haroun,[65] Level V, (Bones).

Level IV Summary

Cognitive Development: The Ability to Recognize that Every Quality of a Thing Represents a Membership in the Class of All Other Things With Those Same Qualities.

Relative to our developing cognitive capability, Idris (Level IV) represents the emerging ability able to use nascent, simple logic. This stage is also known as the stage of classroom consciousness.

Mudghatan is a stage in the humans' developing cognitive capacity for the conscious acquisition and comprehension of knowledge. At this stage, that capacity is partially formed and partially unformed, active but not yet stable and mature.

From a sacred evolutionary perspective, the essence of this state is the transition stage of the original human nature from unconscious to conscious (partly formed and partly unformed).

LEVEL V:

Izaaman: The Logic Tools for Digesting the Knowledge in Matter with a Potential for Error

QURANIC REFERENCES FOR AARON ON LEVEL V OF THE *ISRA WA MI'RAJ*

[Note: Because the key reference for this section, Holy Quran 20:85–20:99, is so extensive, I have discussed it in the tafsir below. I also recommend you refer to your own Qur'an.]

THE HADITH OF AARON ON LEVEL V OF THE *ISRA WA MI'RAJ*

((THEN WE ASCENDED to the fifth heaven and again the same questions and answers were exchanged as in previous heavens. There I met and greeted Aaron who said, 'You are welcomed, O brother, and a Prophet."

IMAM MOHAMMED (RA) ON AARON ON LEVEL V
OF THE *ISRA WA MI'RAJ*
AARON—ERRAND—ERR[66]

"And look at another comparison in the Holy Qur'an in the revelation to us through Muhammed, the Prophet. Of course, [the Night Journey] is the metaphorical picture of the development of human life from dead matter (23:12-14) and then sperm and clot and fetus lump and bones. So the bones are really the fifth level.

On the fifth level he saw Aaron and look at the name, listen to the name Aaron and you can get out of Aaron "a trip." You're just saying that somebody went from one place to another, he ran an errand. It could have been a bad thing (or a good thing), could have been wrong (or right). We don't know what he was doing on the errand. He just went on an errand, right?

So, err is in it, isn't it? Err, to make a mistake, is in it [sound "Erron"] and we know according to the Bible "Aaron erred." Moses was up in the mountain trying to get some help from G-d for them. Aaron let the people influence him to make a golden calf [according to the Bible] to go back to shirk. And in the Qur'an, he responds once he's caught and realizes what he's done. He says, "Please don't grab me by the hair of my beard!" [He's saying] that's where my fault is: my mouth. I just been chattering too much and wasn't obeying. He was a great man with the words. That's why he was selected to talk with Pharaoh and his magicians. So it is our fifth level where we're subject to err. That's why the Prophet (ﷺ) said, "Take care of five before five be your undoing." He gave an indirect reference to the five. The five it's talking about is our five senses.

Habit will take your senses out of the mold and nature that G-d wants them in, and then the very senses that were given to you to help you, they'll become your undoing or your trouble.[67]"

THE QURANIC SIGNIFICANCE FOR AARON ON LEVEL V
OF THE *ISRA WA MI'RAJ*

مُضْغَةً فَخَلَقْنَا ٱلْمُضْغَةَ عِظَٰمًا

23: 14 "...into a lump [of flesh], and We made [from] the lump, bones..."

Izaaman (Bones)

As stated in our introduction, this publication presents the correlation between a specific section of the Holy Qur'an (23:12-23:14) and the events of *the Isra wa Mi'raj* in the life of Prophet Muhammed (ﷺ), the interpretative methodology of Imam W. D. Mohammed (ra; figurative speech in scripture is science), and the established science of human cognitive development.

For Level V, the best approach for reconciling and locating Aaron in this path to human development is through the story in the Holy Qur'an 20:85–20:99. For brevity, we will not detail the Arabic grammar of each of the verses. Through the key terms, their signification as well as the concrete objects (symbols) in the story, the reconciling message, can be extracted, *Bi-idzni-Ilah*.

20: 85. (Allah) said: "We have tested your people in your absence: the Samiri has led them astray."

20: 86. So Moses returned to his people in a state of indignation and sorrow. He said: "O my people! did not your Lord make a handsome promise to you? Did then the promise seem to you long (in coming)? Or did you desire that Wrath should descend from your Lord on you and so you broke your promise to me?"

20: 87. They said: "We broke not the promise to you as far as lay in our power: but we were made to carry the weight of the ornaments of the (whole) people and we threw them (into the fire) and that was what the Samiri suggested.

In the context of our main idea, brain science shows that human beings are protected and aided but sometimes deceived by the natural function of their brains. We grow to trust and depend on past experiences. Level V uses what has come to it from Levels I–IV, just as each subsequent level benefits and functions on the basis of the establishment of the prior level. Figuratively speaking, "the weight of the peoples' ornaments" means carrying things that have proven valuable in the past. Storing and using experience is what the brain does naturally and intuitively. The brain naturally values past experience. The colloquial saying is, "Experience is the best teacher." Our natural tendency is to trust what has been confirmed by broad past, objective experience. But sometimes the right answer and correct perception is counter-intuitive, meaning it runs counter to past experience or what our brains have come to prize. We see this in the story of Moses and the Wiseman in Surah 18.

So from a cognitive science perspective, the transition from Aaron (culturally evolved logic) to Moses (education after error) is like the transition from Yusuf on Level III (pre-concrete operations, five-sense-dependent judgment) to Idris on Level IV (concrete operations, classroom consciousness). Both phases entail learning how to think beyond sensory information and not allow past thoughts and experience to dominate your reasoning.

So the erected golden calf or sacred cow figuratively represent hasty conclusions reached impulsively, based on past valuable knowledge that the person is reluctant to give up. (See Moses, Bani Isra'il and the heifer; 2: 67–2:74).

Focusing on the sound of words, with the *ayn* in *harra*,[68] it connects Aaron (Haroun) with the concepts of rushing and haste in the Quran (11:78 and 37:70). *HaaRa* means "to fall from a high place, to break down and collapse." These meanings also add up to "a logic that failed, a logic that doesn't hold up."

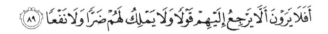

20: 89. Could they not see that it could not return them a word (for answer) and that it had no power either to harm them or to do them good?

As we've said, the transition from Aaron to Moses is like the transition from Yusuf to Idris. This verse implies that they are off the natural sense-based track. It wasn't Aaron, per se, but it was the beginning or even his first watch in the absence of Moses. Never the less, the verse implies that the normal function of the senses in connection with natural reasoning was cut off. So it was at this point undeveloped and immature because, according to the verse, natural sense logic coupled with the firm belief in Allah and the unseen could have helped them naturally reason away the illusion that was being cast by the *Samiri's* beautiful lie.

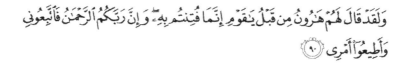

20: 90. Aaron had already before this said to them: "O my people! ye are being tested in this: for verily your Lord is (Allah) Most Gracious: so follow me and obey my command."

This verse provides more supportive implications from the name Haroun. *Harra* (taking the *waw* and *nuun* ending as a pluralizing suffix) leads to *Lane's Lexicon Dictionary* definition, "meat so well cooked that it falls off the bone." (Visually, this is Level V; bones with no flesh.) Aaron is *izaaman* (indefinite bones; higher reasoning that is also a kind of indefinite logic). *Harra* also means "speech with incorrectness" and "the young shoot of a palm tree when plucked from the mother-tree." This can be understood as knowledge from an order above the masses.

20: 91. They had said: "We will not abandon this cult but we will devote ourselves to it until Moses returns to us.

20: 92. (Moses) said: "O Aaron! what kept thee back when thou sawest them going wrong

20: 93. "From following me? Didst thou then disobey my order?"

20: 94. (Aaron replied: "O son of my mother! seize (me not) by my beard nor by (the hair of) my head! Truly I feared lest thou shouldst say `Thou hast caused a division among the Children of Israel and thou didst not respect my word!'"

Aaron knew better, but he didn't have *yaqin* sufficient to protect the body/people from the illusion that had captivated them due to their appetites unchecked by knowledge (the *Samiri*). Figuratively,

Aaron/Haroun's status is analogous to the four-phase movement from unconscious incompetence to unconscious competence.

The people represent the old habits and past experiences. The *Samiri* represents the rationalizations that keeps one stuck in the past. That is a type of "unconscious incompetence". "They don't know and they don't know that they don't know". Aaron represents "conscious incompetence"; the stage where we know more than we are able to perform and when "we are aware after we made an error" in trying to apply what we know. Moses (VI), in that construction, represents "conscious competence" (higher knowledge learned after correction). The ability to apply knowledge correctly but must do so consciously. Abraham (VII) represents "unconscious competence" (universal knowledge operating in and upon the fully developed mind); A person who doesn't "have to think about" the correctness of their actions in the matter "they do the right thing automatically". We hear and we obey!

Aaron's position relative to Moses at this point is as Moses was to Al-Khidr (18:60–18:82); meaning that though Moses had strength in "logic" his logic wasn't yet inspired. Though Aaron represents the newly acquired capability for logic his logic was not yet sound according to revelation.

20: 95. (Moses) said: "What then is thy case O Samiri?"

20: 96. He replied: "I saw what they saw not: so I took a handful (of dust) from the footprint of the Apostle and threw it (into the calf): thus did my soul suggest to me."

The *Samiri* represent the rationalizations we hold that keep us stuck in the past. Aaron represents the learning stage where we gain knowledge from the past but not revealed knowledge. Thus, to that extent, it is what we learned unconsciously. It may or may not be useful or correct. In the absence of Moses (the light of revelation from the top of the mountain; fuller development of our cognitive capacity with the help of G-d's guidance), we are likely to err at first though not intentionally.

The root of the name *Samiri* carries the meaning "a woman with whom you hold lengthy discourse by night." The night represents the unconscious, which is the dwelling place of our unenlightened urges and impulses. Knowledge gained from that discourse can't always be trusted, like moonlight (philosophy) versus sunlight (material science). *Samiri* in this verse fulfills the statement, "It was We who created man and We know what dark suggestions his soul makes to him" (50:16).

> *20: 97. (Moses) said: "Get you gone! but thy (punishment) in this life will be that you wilt say `Touch me not'[69]; and moreover (for a future penalty) you have a promise that will not fail: now look at your god to whom you have become a devoted worshipper: we will certainly (melt) it in a blazing fire and scatter it broadcast in the sea!"*

To reiterate, *harr* means "meat so well cooked that it falls off the bone." It is pluralized to Haroun, and the *Samiri* represents the *sharr* (potential harm) in our growing intellect. *Samiri* is the potential in us that could lead our development astray by being hasty in our reasoning and conclusions and not using G-d's revelation to critique our own logic.

Against Allah's declaration, Iblis hastily concluded before Adam was complete that he was better than Adam. He came to the wrong conclusion. Each of us has a jinn who can also lead us toward wrong conclusions if we are not rightly guided.

> *20: 98. But the god of you all is the One Allah: there is no god but He: all things He comprehends in His knowledge.*

> *20: 99. Thus do We relate to thee some stories of what happened before: for We have sent thee a Message from Our own Presence.*

To address the cognitive skill born on Level V, the mind comes into the capability to do with abstracts/relationships what they were able to do with concretes at Level III. Namely, relating (ideas, words, symbols, etc.) and differentiating abstracts/relationships (ideas, words, symbols, etc.,) upon the basis of a certain logic.

According to cognitive science, one characteristic of this stage of thinking is the emergence of deductive reasoning, which allows the person to logically make inferences between the more general and the less general. For example, consider the following syllogism: "All women are mortal. All queens are women. Thus, all queens are mortal." This is the stage where the brain learns to recognize logical relationships and the logic of and between relationships. Consider the following analogy: "Night is to day as death is to life." Brains in this stage can deduce the relationships between these pairs of opposites.

Essentially, errors are more likely made in the form of fallacious logic or reasoning, because this is the beginning of the mind's ability to deal with abstract concepts. Abstract reasoning and logic is like sailing or flying. It is easy for an unfinished navigator to veer off course and not even recognize it.

AARON IS THE HYOID BONE

20:25. (Moses) said: "O my Lord! expand me my breast;"

20:26. "Ease my task for me;

20:27. "And remove the impediment from my speech.

20:28. "So they may understand what I say:

20:29. "And give me a Minister from my family

20:30. "Aaron my brother;

20:31. "Add to my strength through him

20:32. "And make him share my task:

20:33. "That we may celebrate Thy praise without stint

20:34. "And remember Thee without stint:

20:35. For You are He that (ever) regards us."

20:36. (Allah) said: "Granted is thy prayer O Moses!"

The hyoid bone is the only bone in the human body not connected to another. The significance of that is how it illustrates the truth that this stage of cognitive development, the capacity for making logical connections, has begun, but the connections may not always be sound and valid.

Anatomically, because of where it's located, the hyoid is often considered the anatomical foundation of speech. It can work with the larynx (voice box) and tongue to produce the range of human vocalizations. Imam Mohammed (ra) says, "Scripture will use figurative expressions, figurative speech and abstract symbols to address what is actual and what is scientific, what is very real.[70]" So it is reasonable to represent Aaron, generally, as the bone stage, particularly the hyoid bone.

LEVEL V SUMMARY
COGNITIVE DEVELOPMENT: ABSTRACT RELATIONSHIPS ARE COMPREHENDED AND USED CONCRETELY

Aaron on Level V represents the learning stage where we gain some knowledge from the past but not revealed knowledge. It's what we learned during our socialization and acculturation. Aaron is the personification of culturally evolved logic, which is born on Level V but can only become mature when it is connected with and corrected by revealed knowledge (Moses, Level VI).

LEVEL VI:

Izaaman Lahman: Universal Logic for Particular Culture

Quranic References for Musa/Moses on Level VI of the Isra Wa Mi'raj

۞ وَإِذِ ٱسۡتَسۡقَىٰ مُوسَىٰ لِقَوۡمِهِۦ فَقُلۡنَا ٱضۡرِب بِّعَصَاكَ ٱلۡحَجَرَۖ فَٱنفَجَرَتۡ مِنۡهُ
ٱثۡنَتَا عَشۡرَةَ عَيۡنٗاۖ قَدۡ عَلِمَ كُلُّ أُنَاسٍ مَّشۡرَبَهُمۡۖ كُلُواْ وَٱشۡرَبُواْ مِن رِّزۡقِ ٱللَّهِ وَلَا
تَعۡثَوۡاْ فِي ٱلۡأَرۡضِ مُفۡسِدِينَ ﴿٦٠﴾

2: 60. And remember Moses prayed for water for his people; We said: "Strike the rock with thy staff." Then gushed forth therefrom twelve springs Each group knew its own place for water.[71]"

The Hadith of Musa/Moses on Level VI of the Isra Wa Mi'raj

"Then we ascended to the 6th heaven and again the same questions and answers were exchanged as in the previous heavens. There I met and greeted Moses who said, 'You are welcomed O brother and a Prophet.."[72]

Imam Mohammed (ra) on Musa/Moses on Level VI of the *Isra Wa Mi'raj*

"In the Holy Qur'an is the metaphorical picture of the development of human life from dead matter and then sperm and then clot and fetus lump and bones. So the bone is really the fifth level.

Prophet Aaron, he's in the 5th level representing the five senses, but that level also represents bone, where bone has been formed. That's the level where bones can form. Bones are symbolic of logical connections. The Bible speaks of it in the valley of dead bones and the bones coming together. They are dead, separated, but when you put them together, they get life again...

So it's[73] also logic. It refers to logic and (particularly) culture-evolved logic. Culture in its innocence evolves (a) logic. Then after the bones, we're told by the metaphorical language of Qur'an,[74] "and He clothed the bones with flesh." So, after logic, logic evolves what? Education, classic education. You can't have education without logic. Education must form to logic and that's the 6th level, Moses. Don't the Jews call Moses the teacher? The great teacher of the Jews, Moses, peace be upon him.[75]"

The Quranic Significance for Musa/Moses on Level VI of the *Isra Wa Mi'raj*

فَكَسَوْنَا ٱلْعِظَٰمَ لَحْمًا

23: 14 "...and We covered the bones with flesh..."

Al-Izaama (The Bones) Lahmaan (Flesh)

Level V (Aaron) was the birth of the capability for logic, but it's immature at this stage— un-established and not free from potential error. This is the intellect's capability for logic when it is new to the realm of logical abstraction.[76] From the social perspective, Aaron (Level V) is logic born out of a particular culture. It, too, may be on the right or the wrong foundations (premises, frames of reference, worldview, etc.). Whenever that is the case, the logic must be corrected by an education/logic fit for universal culture–Moses (Level VI). Prototypically, as this revealed schema shows, it's normal that such correction takes place. "Moses is always necessary" in the individual and collective human journey to full human development.

The Stories of Moses are the Reality of Moses

The reality of Moses as one of the sacred properties of human nature evolving to its destiny is well told in the many stories we have of him in the Holy Qur'an. Stories have a special way of connecting with people. They draw them in in a way that other data forms do not. The Scientific American Mind, states

> "Stories summarize and simplify and reduce the dimensionality of complex issues.... Stories may be the only way to get to the heart of really complex situations.... Stories have such a powerful and universal appeal that the neurological roots of both telling tales and enjoying them are probably tied to crucial parts of our social cognition.[77]"

In the conclusion of the last chapter on Aaron, we stated that the hyoid bone is the only bone in the human body not connected to another. We concluded that the significance of that is how it illustrates the truth at stage of cognitive development, wherein there is the capacity to make logical connections, but the connections may not always be sound and valid.

Moses (Level VI) represents the reasoning capability that enables the person to determine whether or not the conclusions derived from the premises are logically sound and valid.[78] More importantly, this is the capability to determine morally, ethically and spiritually if the logic is conducive to the forward progress of the human nature toward its destiny.

Moses represents "immature logic corrected and given the proper rationale," that is, made sound relative to G-d and the nature and destiny of human beings.

This can also be read from Moses' meeting with Al-Khidzr. When Moses met Al-Khidzr, Moses was in his own "Aaron stage." At that stage in his story, Moses was one whose ability to use logic had not become inspired; beyond the concrete ("sought rest on a rock" 18:62-63).

Moses' maturity is illustrated in his defeat of Pharaoh's magician[79]. He used what appeared to be the same magic, but with *taqwa* and in accordance with the guidance of G-d (revealed knowledge) in service of truth and human freedom. His battle with the magicians (snakes vs. snakes) represents the mental battle of rationale vs. rationale, reasoning vs. reasoning. Theirs was from illusion (false reasoning not grounded in truth); his from the revelation of Allah (proofs, credentials, scriptural logic upon the reality of G-d and his revelation). Moses represents the ability to keep one's logic sound and valid and in service to those cultural sensitivities that are intended for man by Allah.

Aaron and Moses have the same mother. Their socialization and sensitivities have the same source. However, Moses is "slightly higher in the *Isra* than Aaron and, therefore, higher in role, status and function." They also stand in the same asymmetrical relationship on the scale of cognitive development for the human being.

The cognitive capability at this level includes combinatorial reasoning, the process of selecting, organizing and reorganizing things or ideas according to one's purpose. For example, organizing or re-organizing books based on size, number of pages, color, content, etc. In science, it applies to forming hypotheses, constructing experiments and evaluating results.

Moses represents the universal logic from the developed human nature, spiritual and scientific, which serves the total need of a particular society.

وَإِذِ ٱسۡتَسۡقَىٰ مُوسَىٰ لِقَوۡمِهِۦ فَقُلۡنَا ٱضۡرِب بِّعَصَاكَ ٱلۡحَجَرَۖ فَٱنفَجَرَتۡ مِنۡهُ
ٱثۡنَتَا عَشۡرَةَ عَيۡنٗاۖ قَدۡ عَلِمَ كُلُّ أُنَاسٖ مَّشۡرَبَهُمۡۖ كُلُواْ وَٱشۡرَبُواْ مِن رِّزۡقِ ٱللَّهِ وَلَا
تَعۡثَوۡاْ فِي ٱلۡأَرۡضِ مُفۡسِدِينَ ٦٠

2: 60. And remember Moses prayed for water for his people; We said: "Strike the rock [logic] with thy staff." Then gushed forth therefrom twelve springs [organized universal spiritual nature; natural governance of universal spirituality]. Each group [particularity] knew its own place for water."[80]

Moses is a type of "universal within the particular." What he represents, in terms of the correction of a culture's logic, is the realignment of the culture's logic with the universal logic (*fitrah*) but within that culture's particular reality.

Regarding the reconstruction of the original human being, Imam Mohammed (ra) said, "I'm giving you a picture, a symbolic picture of a human being. His skeleton is the logic; that is the structure. It shows how it is built up and how it is formed, what kind of shape it takes, and then the meat adheres to that (*Al-Izaama lahmaan*) and then there is a nice human figure."

SUPPLEMENT TO LEVEL VI

There is an illustration from the Quran of immature logic and intellect gone astray:

2: 16. These are they who have bartered guidance for error: but their traffic is profitless and they have lost true direction.

This verse shows that whenever individuals adopt a way of thinking and reasoning that doesn't follow the guidance in nature or in revelation, that thinking is profitless.

2: 17. Their similitude is that of a man who kindled a fire; when it lighted all around him Allah took away their light and left them in utter darkness so they could not see.

"Kindling a fire" means forming rationalizations to justify one's position. This verse speaks to the fact that the "Intellect is the servant of interests." The intellect habitually serves the aspirations of the individual. Whenever the intellect is brought into service for one whose desires are contrary to Allah's will, such persons are "left in utter darkness."

2: 18. Deaf dumb and blind they will not return (to the path).

This verse shows that such individuals have lost the proper use of their natural faculties due to their unrighteous irrationality and, therefore, they've lost the means to be guided to their true destiny.

2: 19. Or (another similitude) is that of a rain-laden cloud from the sky; in it are zones of darkness and thunder and lightning they press their fingers in their ears to keep out the stunning thunder-clap the while they are in terror of death. But Allah is ever round the rejecters of Faith!

This verse reveals the "mental and spiritual condition of such people that fit this description. It's a description of their anxiety when faced with valid deductive arguments, which they fear. Their anxiety is amplified when they're faced with premises they can't comprehend or whose truth they reject. Even so, the inferences and implications from nature and revelation are loud and clear. When such people are confronted with these powerful insights and ideas, they see them as dangerous to their "way of life." So, they turn off their own nature to ease their anxiety.

20: 20. The lightning all but snatches away their sight; every time the light (helps) them they walk therein and when the darkness grows on them they stand still. And if Allah willed He could take away their faculty of hearing and seeing; for Allah hath power over all things.

This verses shows that they have a hypocritical relationship with truth. At the same time that they see the powerful insights and ideas coming from the wisdom of G-d through G-d's agents as dangerous to their "way of life," they use it when it serves their interest but then abandon it again when the guidance contradicts their desires.

Soundness and Validity

Soundness is defined as the quality of being based on valid reasoning or good judgement. Validity is defined as the quality of being logically or factually sound, cogent. What is a valid argument? An argument is valid if (the truth of) the premises logically guarantees (the truth of) the conclusion. A valid argument may still have a false conclusion. For example, consider the following syllogism: "All toasters are items made of gold. All items made of gold are time-travel devices. Therefore, all toasters are time-travel devices." This is valid in as much as the conclusion follows faithfully from the premises, but it is not sound because its premises aren't true.

What is a sound argument? An argument is sound if and only if it is both valid and all of its premises are true. Consider the following example: "No felons are eligible voters. Some professional athletes are felons. Therefore, some professional athletes are not eligible voters."

Level VI Summary

Cognitive Development: Combinatorial Reasoning- Selecting, Organizing and Reorganizing Things or Ideas According to Purpose

Moses (Level VI) represents the reasoning capability that enables the person to determine if the conclusions derived from the premises are logically sound and valid. More importantly, the person develops the capability to determine morally, ethically and spiritually if the logic is conducive to the forward progress of the human nature toward its destiny.

Moses represents "immature logic corrected (Aaron, Level IV) and given the proper rationale," made sound relative to G-d and the nature and destiny of human beings.

Moses represents the universal spiritual logic from the nature that serves the entirety of a particular society.

.

LEVEL VII:

Khalqaan Akhara: "The Standing Place of Abraham" and All That He Represents

Quranic References for Ibrahim/Abraham on Level VII of the Isra Wa Mi'raj

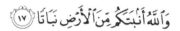

71: 17 "And Allah has caused you to grow from the earth a [progressive] growth."

اَلَمۡ تَرَ إِلَى ٱلَّذِى حَاجَّ إِبۡرَهِۦمَ فِى رَبِّهِۦٓ أَنۡ ءَاتَـٰهُ ٱللَّهُ ٱلۡمُلۡكَ إِذۡ قَالَ إِبۡرَهِۦمُ رَبِّىَ ٱلَّذِى يُحۡىِۦ وَيُمِيتُ قَالَ أَنَا۠ أُحۡىِۦ وَأُمِيتُ قَالَ إِبۡرَهِۦمُ فَإِنَّ ٱللَّهَ يَأۡتِى بِٱلشَّمۡسِ مِنَ ٱلۡمَشۡرِقِ فَأۡتِ بِهَا مِنَ ٱلۡمَغۡرِبِ فَبُهِتَ ٱلَّذِى كَفَرَ وَٱللَّهُ لَا يَهۡدِى ٱلۡقَوۡمَ ٱلظَّـٰلِمِينَ ﴿٢٥٨﴾

2: 258. Have you not considered the one who argued with Abraham about his Lord [merely] because Allah had given him kingship? When Abraham said, "My Lord is the one who gives life and causes death," he said, "I give life and cause death." Abraham said, "Indeed, Allah brings up the sun from the east, so bring it up from the west." So, the disbeliever was overwhelmed [by astonishment], and Allah does not guide the wrongdoing people.

وَإِذْ قَالَ إِبْرَهِيمُ رَبِّ أَرِنِى كَيْفَ تُحْىِ الْمَوْتَى قَالَ أَوَلَمْ تُؤْمِن قَالَ بَلَى وَلَكِن لِيَطْمَئِنَّ قَلْبِى قَالَ فَخُذْ أَرْبَعَةً مِّنَ الطَّيْرِ فَصُرْهُنَّ إِلَيْكَ ثُمَّ اجْعَلْ عَلَى كُلِّ جَبَلٍ مِّنْهُنَّ جُزْءًا ثُمَّ ادْعُهُنَّ يَأْتِينَكَ سَعْيًا وَاعْلَمْ أَنَّ اللَّهَ عَزِيزٌ حَكِيمٌ ﴿٢٦٠﴾

"And when Abraham said (unto his Lord): My Lord! Show me how You give life to the dead, He said: Do you not believe? Abraham said: Yes, but (I ask) in order that my heart may be at ease. (His Lord) said: Take four of the birds and cause them to incline to you, then place a part of them on each hill, then call them, they will come to you in haste, and know that Allah is Mighty, Wise."

وَكَذَلِكَ نُرِى إِبْرَهِيمَ مَلَكُوتَ السَّمَوَاتِ وَالْأَرْضِ وَلِيَكُونَ مِنَ الْمُوقِنِينَ ﴿٧٥﴾

And thus, did We show Abraham the realm of the heavens and the earth that he would be among the certain [in faith]

فَلَمَّا جَنَّ عَلَيْهِ الَّيْلُ رَءَا كَوْكَبًا قَالَ هَذَا رَبِّى فَلَمَّا أَفَلَ قَالَ لَا أُحِبُّ الْآفِلِينَ ﴿٧٦﴾

So, when the night covered him [with darkness], he saw a star. He said, "This is my lord." But when it set, he said, "I like not those that disappear."

فَلَمَّا رَءَا ٱلْقَمَرَ بَازِغًا قَالَ هَٰذَا رَبِّى فَلَمَّآ أَفَلَ قَالَ لَئِن لَّمْ يَهْدِنِى رَبِّى لَأَكُونَنَّ مِنَ ٱلْقَوْمِ ٱلضَّآلِّينَ ﴿٧٧﴾

And when he saw the moon rising, he said, "This is my lord." But when it set, he said, "Unless my Lord guides me, I will surely be among the people gone astray."

فَلَمَّا رَءَا ٱلشَّمْسَ بَازِغَةً قَالَ هَٰذَا رَبِّى هَٰذَآ أَكْبَرُ فَلَمَّآ أَفَلَتْ قَالَ يَٰقَوْمِ إِنِّى بَرِىٓءٌ مِّمَّا تُشْرِكُونَ ﴿٧٨﴾

And when he saw the sun rising, he said, "This is my lord; this is greater." But when it set, he said, "O my people, indeed I am free from what you associate with Allah.

إِنِّى وَجَّهْتُ وَجْهِىَ لِلَّذِى فَطَرَ ٱلسَّمَٰوَٰتِ وَٱلْأَرْضَ حَنِيفًا وَمَآ أَنَا۠ مِنَ ٱلْمُشْرِكِينَ ﴿٧٩﴾

Indeed, I have turned my face toward He who created the heavens and the earth, inclining toward truth, and I am not of those who associate others with Allah."

فِيهِ ءَايَٰتٌۢ بَيِّنَٰتٌ مَّقَامُ إِبْرَٰهِيمَ وَمَن دَخَلَهُۥ كَانَ ءَامِنًا وَلِلَّهِ عَلَى ٱلنَّاسِ حِجُّ ٱلْبَيْتِ مَنِ ٱسْتَطَاعَ إِلَيْهِ سَبِيلًا وَمَن كَفَرَ فَإِنَّ ٱللَّهَ غَنِىٌّ عَنِ ٱلْعَٰلَمِينَ ﴿٩٧﴾

3: 97. In it are clear signs [such as] the standing place of Abraham. And whoever enters it shall be safe. And [due] to Allah from the people is a pilgrimage to the House - for whoever is able to find thereto a way. But whoever disbelieves - then indeed, Allah is free from need of the worlds.

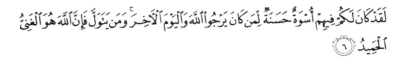

"There has already been for you an excellent pattern in Abraham and those with him."

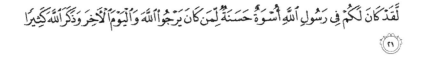

60: 6. "There has certainly been for you in them an excellent pattern for anyone whose hope is in Allah and the Last Day. And whoever turns away - then indeed, Allah is the Free of need, the Praiseworthy."

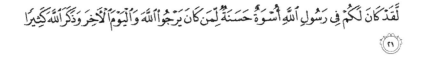

33: 21. "Ye have indeed in the Messenger of Allah a beautiful pattern (of conduct) for any one whose hope is in Allah and the Final Day, and who engages much in the Praise of Allah."

THE HADITH OF ABRAHAM ON LEVEL VII
OF THE *ISRA WA MI'RAJ*

"So, when I went (over the seventh heaven), there I saw Abraham (Ibrahim). Gabriel said to me: 'This is your father; pay your greetings to him.' So, I greeted him and he returned the greetings to me and said: 'You are welcomed, O pious son and pious Prophet.'"[81]

IMAM MOHAMMED (RA) ON ABRAHAM ON LEVEL VII
OF THE *ISRA WA MI'RAJ*

"And the seventh level is Ibrahim our father, another father, our second father Abraham and this level in the development or ascension or growth pattern for the intellect, showing the growth pattern for the intellect in its interaction with the material world. It cannot have any growth unless it has interaction with the material world. You put the seed in the ground and then it can have life. So man's mind has to impregnate the matter; the knowledge body of matter. It must go in there and then he can have growth; life.

The teaching needs to serve human life. [As man's knowledge grows] this knowledge branches off into certain special fields and becomes special disciplines, specialized knowledge, right? And it leaves the main purpose of the knowledge. And the main purpose of the knowledge is to edify human excellence, life, give construction to it so that it can have its reward that G-d intended for it in the society of human beings. That's the purpose of it [i.e., education, teaching, knowledge]. All these other things are fringe benefits. The electric fan or the central heating and cooling in the house. All these are fringe benefits of it, but some will take their minds to these special fields and they leave the main path for this development and they punish the human life in ignorance, but finally they all [i.e., education, teaching, knowledge] have to be reconciled with the human person, don't they?

We see that now, what they call urbanization, urban renewal. Looking back at it, we see many mistakes that were made. It was not done with a conscious awareness of what human life is asking for.[82]

So a big mistake was made and I'm giving that just as a helper to help us see how civilizations of the world have erred and have gone into sciences and this and that and have lost focus on what is more important, and that is to free man and structure man in his life and society so that he realizes the best conditions intended for him by G-d through matter, you see?

Abraham, then, represents the focus in knowledge to keep knowledge whole and it says, 'Keep my Sabbath whole, seventh day.' So Abraham represents the focus for keeping it whole. He's the universal thinker. His heart is universal, his intellect, spirit is universal, and G-d says that he fulfills his debt to G-d.

On this level, what is he? He's knowledge that preserves what is universal, and in his universal composition, it aids and helps and corrects that, that is local, keeps it from going astray so he is really the universal teacher.

Moses is the intellect that teaches, but teaches for a particular need and particular people, particular situation, not the whole world. Abraham is the teacher for the whole world, not for any nation. He actually left his nation. He was a national citizen under the rule of his father. He broke with it, he left his nation and finally G-d called him. He said, You're going to be My leader of the nations, isn't it wonderful?[83]"

THE QURANIC SIGNIFICANCE
OF ABRAHAM ON LEVEL VII OF THE *ISRA WA MI'RAJ*

ثُمَّ أَنشَأْنَهُ خَلْقًا ءَاخَرَ

23: 14. "...then We developed it into another creation..."
KhalqaanAkhara

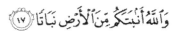

71: 17. "And Allah has caused you to grow from the earth a [progressive] growth."

This verse is literally and figuratively a narrative and symbolic expression of the entire process of physical, mental and spiritual development that this publication is dedicated to unveiling. The chapter number (71) and verse number (17) are a palindrome, which signifies that "the beginning is the end and the end is the beginning." The plant's seed is a symbol for Adam, the natural human being and all of its potential, evolving up to Abraham. Abraham is the realized capability for divine communication through which the human being evolves to the height of revelation.

The 71 contains the seven biological movements, from "quintessence of clay"/Adam (23:12) up to the formation of "another creation"/ Abraham (23:14), all working together to produce a functional human brain. The 17 portrays the functional human brain, which proceeds up through its seven cognitive movements.

Imam Mohammed (ra) identifies these two sacred movements. He said, "One father, Adam, followed the nature. The other father, Abraham, followed the direction in the intelligence. One father, Adam, fathered the direction in the nature. The other father, Abraham, fathered the direction in the intelligence."[84] Abraham is the personification of the activities in the mind of the free thinker who will take the world where it has to go—rationally, intellectually and spiritually.[85]

IBRAHIM (ABRAHAM) IS THE DEVOUTLY OBEDIENT INTELLECT OF MAN

"Anas b. Malik reported that a person came to Allah's Messenger (may peace be upon him) and said: O, *The best of creation*; thereupon Allah's Messenger (may peace be upon him) said: He ["The best of creation"] is Ibrahim (peace be upon him).[86]"

Abu Huraira reported the Prophet (ﷺ) said, "Allah (swt) created the intellect, He told it to stand up and it did so, then told it to turn its back and it did so, then told it to turn its face and it did so, then told it to sit and it did so. He then said *I have created nothing better or more excellent or finer than you*. By you I shall receive, by you I shall give, by you I shall know, by you I shall reprove, by you reward will be gained and by opposing you, punishment will be received.[87]"

In the two above reports, one expresses that Ibrahim was "the best of creation" and the other says, "There is nothing better or more excellent that the intellect." Consequently, Ibrahim becomes the personification of the devoutly obedient intellect.

There are three events in the Holy Qur'an that can be used to illustrate how Ibrahim is the personification of the devoutly obedient intellect. They are as follows:

The first is revealed in Chapter 21 verses 51–70. In these verses, Abraham, as a youth, smashes the idols in secret, then challenges his people to ask the big idol to reveal who did it. When the people are shamed by this youth into acknowledging that their idols were no G-ds, they put him in the fire. The fire should be understood as their anger and heated arguments and debates against his beliefs. But the fire (their stratagems, thinking and arguments) were "cool and peaceful" for Ibrahim because his sound belief in the one and true G-d insulated him from any of their effects.

The second event comes when Ibrahim had the mental battle with Nimrod. His reasoning and scientific insight confounded Nimrod.

أَلَمۡ تَرَ إِلَى ٱلَّذِى حَآجَّ إِبۡرَٰهِـۧمَ فِى رَبِّهِۦٓ أَنۡ ءَاتَىٰهُ ٱللَّهُ ٱلۡمُلۡكَ إِذۡ قَالَ إِبۡرَٰهِـۧمُ رَبِّىَ ٱلَّذِى يُحۡىِۦ وَيُمِيتُ قَالَ أَنَا۠ أُحۡىِۦ وَأُمِيتُۖ قَالَ إِبۡرَٰهِـۧمُ فَإِنَّ ٱللَّهَ يَأۡتِى بِٱلشَّمۡسِ مِنَ ٱلۡمَشۡرِقِ فَأۡتِ بِهَا مِنَ ٱلۡمَغۡرِبِ فَبُهِتَ ٱلَّذِى كَفَرَۗ وَٱللَّهُ لَا يَهۡدِى ٱلۡقَوۡمَ ٱلظَّـٰلِمِينَ ۝

2: 258. Have you not considered the one who argued with Abraham about his Lord [merely] because Allah had given him kingship? When Abraham said, "My Lord is the one who gives life and causes death," he said, "I give life and cause death." Abraham said, "Indeed, Allah brings up the sun from the east, so bring it up from the west." So the disbeliever was overwhelmed [by aston-ishment], and Allah does not guide the wrongdoing people.

A third example is in the Holy Qur'an 2:260. This verse shows that Ibrahim's *qalb* (i.e., heart; the seat of affection and understanding) was searching for "a concrete way of understanding his belief in the resurrection."

وَإِذْ قَالَ إِبْرَٰهِۦمُ رَبِّ أَرِنِى كَيْفَ تُحْىِ ٱلْمَوْتَىٰ قَالَ أَوَلَمْ تُؤْمِنْ قَالَ بَلَىٰ وَلَٰكِن
لِّيَطْمَئِنَّ قَلْبِى قَالَ فَخُذْ أَرْبَعَةً مِّنَ ٱلطَّيْرِ فَصُرْهُنَّ إِلَيْكَ ثُمَّ ٱجْعَلْ عَلَىٰ كُلِّ جَبَلٍ مِّنْهُنَّ
جُزْءًا ثُمَّ ٱدْعُهُنَّ يَأْتِينَكَ سَعْيًا وَٱعْلَمْ أَنَّ ٱللَّهَ عَزِيزٌ حَكِيمٌ ۝

2: 260. "And when Abraham said (unto his Lord): My Lord! Show me how You give life to the dead, He said: Do you not believe? Abraham said: Yes, but (I ask) in order that my heart may be at ease. (His Lord) said: Take four of the birds and cause them to incline to you, then place a part of them on each hill, then call them, they will come to you in haste, and know that Allah is Mighty, Wise."

This scientific experiment in service to abstract reasoning and is enough to satisfy Ibrahim's heart, mind and soul. This is so because Ibrahim has and represents both faith and intellect, mature and reconciled, the highest level of abstract reasoning with faith in service to Allah. Ibrahim represents the fullness of our human capacity for abstract reasoning. Imam Mohammed (ra) speaks to the importance of abstract reasoning:

> *"Now I have to explain this to you, but there are among you many in the audience and behind you that understand abstract reasoning. Abstract reasoning uses concretes to talk about that which is not concrete. It uses physical things like this to talk about something that is not physical. So it will use a physical thing to talk about your spirit, a physical thing to talk about your moral life, a physical thing to talk about your mentality life or your mental makeup. It will use physical things to talk about things that are not tangible, not touchable, not physical. So this is abstract reasoning. I may say to you that a lot of esoteric language is abstract reasoning (or) has abstract reasoning, metaphysics. These languages that use the material to address the non-material are using abstract reasoning if it follows that kind of logic.[88]"*

The human cognitive capability at this stage is being capable of seeing abstracts in concrete ways. Abraham is the beginning of a new life that comes at the end of a prior evolution (*khalqaan akhar*/another creature, 23:14). Abraham is the beginning and the end of our life as thinking creatures.

Imam Mohammed (ra) says, "All human life begins as a thinker.... Our thinking takes patterns and if we do not have an orientation that has as its source matter in the real, natural world creation; if we do not have our [thinking] beginning there, then we [will] take patterns sometimes that are faulty from the beginning. One faulty pattern follows another and most people are just creatures of random thoughts and random patterns of development for the growth of their mind or mentality. That is why the world is in such a mess."[89]

The natural world pattern taken by Abraham, as *khalqaan akhar*/another creature, is revealed in Chapter 6, verses 75-79:

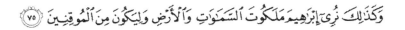

وَكَذَٰلِكَ نُرِىٓ إِبْرَٰهِيمَ مَلَكُوتَ ٱلسَّمَٰوَٰتِ وَٱلْأَرْضِ وَلِيَكُونَ مِنَ ٱلْمُوقِنِينَ ﴿٧٥﴾

Sahih International 6: 75. And thus did We show Abraham the realm of the heavens and the earth that he would be among the certain [in faith].

فَلَمَّا جَنَّ عَلَيْهِ ٱلَّيْلُ رَءَا كَوْكَبًا قَالَ هَٰذَا رَبِّى فَلَمَّآ أَفَلَ قَالَ لَآ أُحِبُّ ٱلْءَافِلِينَ ﴿٧٦﴾

Sahih International 6: 76. So when the night covered him [with darkness], he saw a star. He said, "This is my lord." But when it set, he said, "I like not those that disappear."

فَلَمَّا رَءَا ٱلْقَمَرَ بَازِغًا قَالَ هَٰذَا رَبِّى فَلَمَّآ أَفَلَ قَالَ لَئِن لَّمْ يَهْدِنِى رَبِّى لَأَكُونَنَّ مِنَ ٱلْقَوْمِ ٱلضَّآلِّينَ ﴿٧٧﴾

Sahih International 6: 77. And when he saw the moon rising, he said, "This is my lord." But when it set, he said, "Unless my Lord guides me, I will surely be among the people gone astray."

فَلَمَّا رَءَا الشَّمْسَ بَازِغَةً قَالَ هَذَا رَبِّي هَذَآ أَكْبَرُ فَلَمَّا أَفَلَتْ قَالَ يَنقَوْمِ إِنِّي بَرِىٓءٌ مِّمَّا تُشْرِكُونَ ٧٨

Sahih International 6: 78. And when he saw the sun rising, he said, "This is my lord; this is greater." But when it set, he said, "O my people, indeed I am free from what you associate with Allah.

إِنِّي وَجَّهْتُ وَجْهِيَ لِلَّذِي فَطَرَ السَّمَوَتِ وَالْأَرْضَ حَنِيفًا وَمَآ أَنَا مِنَ الْمُشْرِكِينَ ٧٩

Sahih International 6: 79. Indeed, I have turned my face toward He who created the heavens and the earth, inclining toward truth, and I am not of those who associate others with Allah."

The events in these verses are the figurative expression of what the evolving human being, as a new creature, must do in order to grow further and reach its full development. Developmental scientists describe the human cognitive capability at this stage as follows:

> "The person is able to develop a framework based on a logical rationale about relationships among objects or ideas in the framework, while at the same time realizing that the arrangement is one of many possible ones that eventually may be changed based on fresh insights."[90]

Changing based on fresh insights is precisely what Abraham does in this sequence of verses. First, he observes a phenomenon, comes to a conclusion about it, then changes his conclusion when faced with fresh insights. These verses typify the historic pattern for the growth of science in the world since man became a thinker. These verses neatly encapsulate the scientific history of modern man.

Abraham	Reigning Scientific Theory[91]
Star	Greek Philosophy (@300 B.C.– @500 A.D.)
Moon	Newtonian Physics (@1687–@1915 "Einstein")
Sun	Quantum Physics (@1900–Present)
Tauhid/Yaqin	Material Science + Revelation[92] (Present – Future)

THE MODERN WORLD IS PULLING INTO "THE STANDING PLACE OF ABRAHAM"

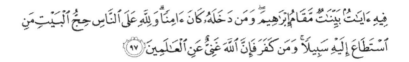

3: 97. In it are clear signs [such as] the standing place of Abraham. And whoever enters it shall be safe. And [due] to Allah from the people is a pilgrimage to the House - for whoever is able to find thereto a way. But whoever disbelieves - then indeed, Allah is free from need of the worlds.

There is an Oriental proverb that states, "The journey of 1000 miles begins with one step." The above verse is the capstone of the entire journey that began with *sullalatim min teen* (23:12). It effectively speaks to the goal state of the entire project of the human being on earth.

While this is not the publication for the full elaboration on the master narrative of Allah's plan for man, we can extract from the parts present in this verse the outline that it gives for the great story of man on earth. This verse is speaking of the sacred precincts that signify the human destiny intended by Allah. It's addressing it much more as an abstract destination as opposed to the geographical location. The Quran says, "In it are clear signs [such as] the standing place of Abraham."

It means that one of the greatest significations of the sacred precincts (which include Zam Zam, Safa and Marwa and the Ka'aba) is the *Maqamu Ibrahim* (the standing place of Abraham.) When we read that sign in the light of the journey/thesis of this publication, it means that it is the destiny. It speaks to the will of Allah who created us "*fi ahasanati taqwim*" (in the most excellent upright mold and structure). It addresses our anthropological evolution to Homo erectus as well as Homo sapiens. Abraham is the representative of the attainment of full human stature, physically, rationally and spiritually.[93] Our human goal is to come to take the stand that Abraham took, physically, rationally and spiritually.

So Allah says, "*wa lillahi ala an-nassi Hijjul baiti*" (and to Allah are all human beings obligated to make pilgrimage there). This is not speaking only to Muslims nor only about the physical visit to Mecca. It is speaking to the will of Allah operating in the nature of creation and in all human beings to come into the physical, rational and spiritual condition that would lead their soul to full development. That would allow them to live in their separate locations but still experience the same rites and disposition displayed on Hajj (2:197). Hajj is a significant expression of the answer to Jesus' prayer, "Thy kingdom come. Thy will be done. On Earth as it is in Heaven."

The verse concludes "*wa man kafara fa inna-llaha ghaniyyun annil aa-lamin*" (and whoever rejects faith; Surely, Allah is self-sufficient needing nothing from his creations). Intuition also leads us to not just see that last statement as an indictment upon those who reject faith. It is also a statement that speaks to what it takes to get to the standing place of Abraham because the verse also says, "*mani sta-ta-a ilayhi sabillan*" (whoever is able to find a way to it.)

What is the way to the standing place of Abraham? It is to come into his example, his posture, his model, even his *uswah* of faith. In the Holy Qur'an 60:4, we find the following two verses:

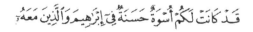

60: 4. "There has already been for you an excellent pattern in Abraham and those with him."

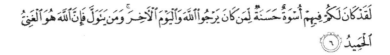

لَّقَدْ كَانَ لَكُمْ فِيهِمْ أُسْوَةٌ حَسَنَةٌ لِّمَن كَانَ يَرْجُواللَّهَ وَالْيَوْمَ الْآخِرَ وَمَن يَتَوَلَّ فَإِنَّ اللَّهَ هُوَ الْغَنِيُّ الْحَمِيدُ ٦

60: 6. "There has certainly been for you in them an excellent pattern for anyone whose hope is in Allah and the Last Day. And whoever turns away - then indeed, Allah is the Free of need, the Praiseworthy."

We see the same meaning with practically the exact same wording in the Holy Qur'an 33:21.

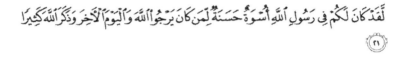

لَّقَدْ كَانَ لَكُمْ فِي رَسُولِ اللَّهِ أُسْوَةٌ حَسَنَةٌ لِّمَن كَانَ يَرْجُواللَّهَ وَالْيَوْمَ الْآخِرَ وَذَكَرَ اللَّهَ كَثِيرًا ٢١

33: 21. "Ye have indeed in the Messenger of Allah a beautiful pattern (of conduct) for anyone whose hope is in Allah and the Final Day, and who engages much in the Praise of Allah."

The path to the standing place of Abraham is the model example of Abraham, who, as this last set of verses shows, is also the model example of Prophet Muhammed (ﷺ). The way to the standing place is by hoping to achieve the human destiny, believing in Allah, and praising him often.

Those who don't reach the standing place of Abraham are those who don't hope to achieve the human destiny, don't believe in Allah, and don't practice praising G-d. That human destiny is not exclusively a place in the hereafter, but it is a physical, rational and spiritual destiny in this life.

The culmination of all human development is seen in the living person of Prophet Muhammed (ﷺ). He is the ultimate signification of all the prophets in the *Isra' wa Mi'raj*, which concludes with Prophet Ibrahim.

LEVEL VII SUMMARY

COGNITIVE DEVELOPMENT: THE ABILITY TO DEVELOP A FRAMEWORK BASED ON A LOGICAL RATIONALE ABOUT RELATIONSHIPS AMONG OBJECTS OR IDEAS IN THE FRAMEWORK

Abraham (Level VII) represents the human cognitive capability to conceptualize abstracts in concrete ways. At this stage of development, humans develops the ability to put abstracts together, formulate a conception and then analyze that conception. If the conception proves to be incorrect, they are capable of reconstructing another conception until they come to the correct conclusion or solution. This level of discernment is the fulfillment of complex human thinking. Abraham represents the beginning of a new life that comes at the end of all prior evolution (*khalqaan akhar*/another creature, 23:14). He is the beginning and end of our life as thinking creatures. He represents the level that brings the realization of the human capability for divine communication through which the human being evolves to the height of revelation and the object of their destiny.

.

LEVEL VIII:

Prophet Muhammed Achieving The Destiny in This Life Through The Application Of The Isra Wa Mi'raj

THE HOLY QUR'AN AND THE LAST PROPHET ARE THE EPITOME OF THE PLAN OF ALLAH

L EVEL VIII IS incorporated here as it is a part of the interpretive insights of Imam Mohammed (ra). In the history of the Prophet, we know that the *Isra Wa Mi'raj* came after the Year of Grief. The Year of Grief was the time immediately following the boycott of the Prophet's tribe, Muslim and non-Muslim, the death of Khadijah (ra), the death of Abu Talib and the incident of At-Ta'if.

After the occasion of the *Isra Wa Mi'raj*, Prophet Muhammed, accompanied by Abu Bakr(ra), made Hijrah to Yathrib, which would become Medinah.

The significance of this is that Prophet Muhammed's completeness in guidance was confirmed and consolidated with the Night Journey, and Allah had prepared a place for him, in freedom, to establish the model community on earth. That crowning event was "the last brick," so to speak. It was the fulfillment in his time of "Thy kingdom come, thy will be done." It also fulfills *"Khalifatul Ard."*

There is so very much that could be elaborated on and, *insha'Allah,* it will be in the future. But in this connection with Level VIII, we must mention John 3:13 "No one has ascended to heaven except He who descended from heaven, even the Son of Man who is in heaven."

"Ascending to heaven" can be read as achieving "the destiny" for man on earth, but that can only be realized after the person "descended from heaven"(something like the *Saa'ee* from Safa and Marwa) by making two cycles: (#1) "rises up through all 7 stages of their human development" and then (#2) "come down" and apply that development in the world. So, 7 (ascend) has to become 8 (descend).

There is one hadith that encapsulates the entire subject and object of the mission of Abraham, all the prophets on earth and of Al-Islam and the conclusion of Allah's plan in Prophet Muhammed (pbuh). It is as follows:

حَدَّثَنَا قُتَيْبَةُ بْنُ سَعِيدٍ، حَدَّثَنَا إِسْمَاعِيلُ بْنُ جَعْفَرٍ، عَنْ عَبْدِ اللَّهِ بْنِ دِينَارٍ، عَنْ أَبِي صَالِحٍ، عَنْ أَبِي هُرَيْرَةَ ـ رضى الله عنه ـ أَنَّ رَسُولَ اللَّهِ صلى الله عليه وسلم قَالَ " إِنَّ مَثَلِي وَمَثَلَ الأَنْبِيَاءِ مِنْ قَبْلِي كَمَثَلِ رَجُلٍ بَنَى بَيْتًا فَأَحْسَنَهُ وَأَجْمَلَهُ، إِلاَّ مَوْضِعَ لَبِنَةٍ مِنْ زَاوِيَةٍ، فَجَعَلَ النَّاسُ يَطُوفُونَ بِهِ وَيَعْجَبُونَ لَهُ، وَيَقُولُونَ هَلاَّ وُضِعَتْ هَذِهِ اللَّبِنَةُ قَالَ فَأَنَا اللَّبِنَةُ، وَأَنَا خَاتِمُ النَّبِيِّينَ " .

Narrated Abu Huraira:
Allah's Messenger (ﷺ) said,

> *"My similitude in comparison with the other prophets before me, is that of a man who has built a house nicely and beautifully, except for a place of one brick in a corner. The people go about it and wonder at its beauty, but say: 'Would that this brick be put in its place!' So, I am that brick, and I am the last of the Prophets."*

The meaning that comes readily to mind from this hadith is that the man who built the building is Ibrahim. Though we know the Qur'an says, "And remember Ibrahim and Isma`il raised the foundations of the House," in this connection, they both are a composite of one rationally and spiritually developed man. The building they built refers to the Kaaba. B'y its significance, it represents the sacred destiny of all human beings.

According to the hadith, the building was perfect except for the absence of one brick. This reveals to us that the historic line of revelation and prophets fostered the perfection of the sacred destiny of the human being, individually and collectively. That history and unfolding of revelation and prophethood evolves the human being, but the evolution is incomplete until the coming of the last of them, Prophet Muhammed. He said, "I am that brick," meaning he completes the objective of divine history. The final revelation of the Holy Qur'an and the life of Prophet Muhammed (ﷺ) are the epitome of the plan of Allah for humanity and society.

THE SCIENCE OF THE ORIGINAL NATURE IS THE CORNERSTONE FOR SOCIETY

The Prophet (ﷺ) said, "If you want to see Abraham, then look at your companion (i.e., the Prophet).[94] Prophet Muhammed (ﷺ) is the reality of Ibrahim. The hadith of 'a man who built a building' calls forth the occasion when Muhammad ibn Abdullah, Al-Amin, placed the black stone in its original place after the rebuilding of the Kaaba. This act was done in fulfillment of previous scripture. The Bible says, "The Stone that the builders rejected has become the head of the corner."[95]

The common Arabic word for brick is *tubah*. The root of the term for brick is *labinah*, the same as the term for milk (*laban*). What is the relationship between milk and brick? It's defined by two other hadith. One hadith is from the *Isra wa Mi'raj* and the other is from a dream of the Prophet (ﷺ).

> During the Isra wa Mi'raj, the Prophet (ﷺ) was brought two bowls; one of them had wine and the other had milk. He was told, "Have either of them!" The Prophet (ﷺ) chose the milk. Jibril said to the Prophet (ﷺ), "*You chose*

the fitrah (original nature); if you had chosen the wine, your ummah would have gone astray after you. You were led to the fitrah (original nature) by choosing the milk; your ummah was led to the original, natural state, too. Wine was rendered haram for you!"

Another hadith tells the story of Prophet Muhammed drinking a bowl of milk in a dream.

Narrated Ibn 'Umar: I heard Prophet Muhammed saying, "While I was sleeping, I was given a bowl full of milk (in a dream), and I drank of it to my fill until I noticed its wetness coming out of my nails, and then I gave the rest of it to 'Umar." They (the people) asked, "What have you interpreted (about the dream)? O Prophet?" He said, "(It is religious) knowledge.⁹⁶"

So, the brick is the science of the original nature as the cornerstone for society. That was realized in the person and work of Prophet Muhammed.

Imam W. D. Mohammed sums it up:

"When G-d said, 'I am going to put a ruler in the earth,' look at how long it took to materialize that. In Prophet Muhammed (ﷺ), it is materialized. Now, we know others were given inspiration from G-d, [but] none of them were able to come into the next life on this earth."⁹⁷ ⁹⁸

Level VIII: :
Prophet Muhammed (ﷺ): The Imam of the Prophets- "The Application of the Science: The Completion of the Whole"

"Amr b. Hishām—Makhlad—Saʿīd b. ʿAbd al-ʿAzīz—Yazīd b. Abī Mālik —the Messenger of God, who said: I was brought a mount larger than a donkey and smaller than a mule, its step at the limit of its sight. I rode it, and Gabriel was with me. I went, and then [Gabriel] said, 'Descend and pray.'

So I did. Then he asked, 'Do you know where you prayed? You prayed at *Tayba* [Medina], the destination of the emigration.'

Then he said, 'Descend and pray.' So I prayed, and he said, 'Do you know where you prayed? You prayed at Mount Sinai where Moses spoke with God.'

Then [later] he said, 'Descend and pray,' so I descended and prayed. He said, 'Do you know where you prayed? You prayed in Bethlehem, where Jesus was born.'

Then I entered the house of sanctity [Jerusalem], where the prophets were assembled for me. Gabriel advanced me forward, so that I led them [in ritual prayers]. Then I was caused to ascend."

Imam Mohammed's commentary from the 1999 Randolph, Virginia, Imam's Retreat explains that there is a Level VIII of human development, which is represented in Prophet Muhammed. His commentary on that point is so clear and comprehensive that it requires little elaboration.

He said,

"Now Muhammad (ﷺ) was shown by G-d the way up through these levels, and on each level he'd greet to show what his relationship was to each one of them. He greeted father (the first man) then brother, brother, and when he got to Abraham he greeted him father and then he led his two fathers [Adam and Abraham] and all of them, including Christ Jesus, in prayer.

Prophet Muhammad (ﷺ) leads them in prayer, and [in the hadith] he said that a building was being constructed and G-d sent His servants to make a contribution to the construction of that building and there was only one stone left out. The place to understand that is the context of revelation. For everything that comes in revelation, the place to understand it is in the context of revelation, not outside of it.

The Bible says there was a stone that the builders rejected.[99] It was not the builders chosen by G-d, but those who were following their way in the world. They sought to build a house and rejected the main stone. It was the cornerstone.... It sets the pattern so that everything is in balance and bears correct relationship; conforms to a pattern. So, it's the beginning in the pattern to form the right angle. And it's called right angle, that's a hint right there. You form the right angle first."

The Cornerstone That the Builders Rejected Was the Innocent Human Heart

"The black stone represents the human heart. Now, we know the heart outside of the body, dead, turns black.

The black stone is symbolic of the heart dead to the life of the human body and to the biological life, and that's exactly what you have to do. This message is given in the Bible in many, many ways, such as the empty vessels. It means minds that have rejected their own authority to think for themselves, that refuse to think for themselves. They ask G-d to tell them how they should form their thoughts in their minds.

So the heart that is dead [the black stone] means there is no more hungering for anything of man's life or of his body, his nature, or his life. He's hungering only for G-d to give it life. So when that happens, G-d responds and gives it light. Now it becomes the cornerstone in the building. It's the heart that is dead [the black stone] that is the requirement for the beginning for the construction of "the life," isn't that true? The requirement is that you first give up your position. Your thinking must die.

And thinking is first in the heart. The heart is the seat of thoughts. You don't think until you want something. That's why the Bible says, 'As a man thinketh in heart, so is he.[100]'

The heart is symbolic of the appetites for the whole life. If we're hungry for food, it bothers our heart if we can't get it. If we're hungry for clothing, it bothers our heart if we can't get it. This goes for anything you hunger for.

Muhammad the Prophet is the one who brings that stone [i.e., the innocent human heart] that was left out of the building and he puts it in its place. Now, isn't that what he did? The chiefs asked him because they trusted him to show them how they all could share the honor of carrying that stone back. So they each grabbed a corner of the cloth and the stone was placed in the cloth. When they got it there, they selected him to be the one to put it in its place so they wouldn't have any problem.[101] So he took his hand [and put the stone back in its place].

So this [black stone/cornerstone] was the [original] human nature—Adam, the Adam that G-d made in his original state. That's what that black stone is. And didn't Muhammad put him [the innocent human nature] back in its proper place and give it back its proper respect? G-d revealed to Muhammad that Adam didn't sin with an intent.[102] He erred and he didn't give up the direction in his life. His nature brought him to meet a word from his G-d and when he saw the word, he repented and G-d accepted his repentance.[103]

So man does not sin by the nature given to him by G-d; he sins by the nature given to him from the errant world.[104] Muhammad put Adam back in his proper place in the dignity and the construction of the house [i.e., civilization]. He put me and you and all the children of Adam back in our proper place, that's what G-d says. He honored all of them, every one.[105]

You see why he leads the seven in prayer? He's the last. He's the leader of mankind, the leader of the history of mankind. He's the leader in human history in the development of man's intellect, his emotional nature and everything, including civilization. Muhammad is the last one and the leader. He is the aim that all of them had and he is the object that all of them were seeking. That is completeness, not just perfection. They all were perfect in their creation, but not completeness. They were seeking completeness and that was only Muhammad the last Prophet that brought the world to completeness [see hadith above], *Allahu Akbar.*

Prophet Muhammad, he's the leader that G-d chose to guide mankind, the world, into light and freedom. Freedom in the classic sense. The classic sense is referring to the needs of the human mind and intellect to accommodate his life in society.

So 'eight holds up the throne' refers to Prophet Muhammad. Firstly, let's look at Prophet Muhammad. Prophet Muhammad (ﷺ) is the eighth one in that picture that we get of the ascension of man and he becomes the leader of that [progression]. He's liberated; freed. He's freed from that progression. We may say that seven gave birth to him. Seven gave birth to the eighth with the creation and guidance of G-d.

Muhammad the Prophet (ﷺ) represents the application of the knowledge and he represents what has to happen to keep that Sabbath, knowledge whole, and by whole is to say, whole meaning keep it consistent. Consistent means one part of it does not hurt the other part, but the parts complement each other. They complement each other so that they lend support to each other without being in conflict with each other. That's what we mean by consistent.[106]

Prophet Muhammad (ﷺ) represents freedom from dependency on the potential in man, to liberate man. Muhammad gets revelation from G-d for the whole life of man, not for one level, but for all the levels for the whole capacity; the whole potential of man. He gets the revelation for that. He gets guidance for that. So, now man does not have to depend upon his own potential or upon his own life to advance the life [the sacred human nature].

Seven signifies completion of knowledge [Abraham]. Eight is application of knowledge [Muhammed].... Now here comes the final revelation complete for the whole life of man and he comes down and begins applying that. He didn't apply it until he came down. Then he went to Medinah. That's when he begins to apply it. So, he comes down and he begins to apply that knowledge with him that is for the whole life of man and society on this earth, humanity.[107] He begins to apply it. That's the eight. The application is the eight. The completion of the knowledge is the seventh, the application of that completion, that wholeness, is the eight.

It answers, 'How do you apply it?' His sunnah enabled him to apply it. G-d chose him because of his *uswaa hasana*; his very perfect and balanced symmetry. And we know Abraham had that same because he wouldn't be called the upright if he didn't have it.[108]

So Muhammad the Prophet (ﷺ), began the 8th. He's the one that established the prayer for us and G-d said establish prayer for My remembrance [*aqamis salate li dhikre*][109] so that they will remember Me. How is G-d remembered? G-d is remembered when we remember

His words to us. That's the best way to remember G-d, by remembering His words to us and in our prayer we recite the Qur'an. The words of G-d to us by way of Jibril the Great Angel and Muhammed the Prophet (ﷺ).

And in the prayer, he gave us the *sajdah*, didn't he? We know the *sajdah* was done by Prophets before. The Bible has Jesus doing *sajdah*,[110] but Muhammad (ﷺ) established it. It wasn't made an institution or an established practice until Muhammad the Prophet. He said the position of *sajdah* is the best position of the *salat*.

$$\text{(أَقْرَبُ مَا يكونُ العَبْدُ مِن رَبِّهِ وَهُوَ سَاجِدٌ ،}$$

$$\text{فَأَكْثِرُوا الدُّعَاءَ) .}$$

"The nearest a slave of Allah is to his Rabb (Lord) is in the state of *Sujood* (Prostration) so increase the Dua (that you make to Allah)." (Sahih Muslim)

Imam Mohammed said, "In *Sujood*, eight points of the human body are touching the ground. [We become] grounded, right? The open hands (2), the forehead (3), the nose (4), the two knees (6) and toes of each foot (8 points). There's a lot of symbolism in this and it is a reference to Muhammad as the 8th in that picture, the *Isra wa Mi'raj* [when he led all of the prophets in prayer]. It shows us the ascension of human essence."

What Allah has revealed to us through the *Isra wa Mi'raj* is the clear path to human development expressed scientifically in scriptural language.

Insha'Allah, we have laid out the stages of development, from the simplest and most fundamental nature of the human being to the full expression of our G-d given human cognitive capabilities. Our sacred human movement begins with Adam and ends with Abraham. Our true human evolution, described in the Prophet's miraculous journey, is the divine expression of the human intellect growing from simple to complex.

The model that Prophet Muhammed established in Medina is the prime example of how those developments are to be lived out in principle wherever human beings may be.

Insha'Allah, institutional educators will see that the elaboration of this material can provide the basis for a curriculum and for content that is in accord with the nature and needs of all human beings.

Allah Knows Best.

ABOUT THE AUTHOR
Imam Faheem Shuaibe

FAHEEM SHUAIBE IS a thought provoking leader and has been the Resident Imam of Masjidul Waritheen in Oakland, California for 34 years. A lifelong student of Imam W. Deen Mohammed (ra), Imam Faheem's unique ability to take complex ideas and make them relatable has led to him serving as a frequently requested presenter at major national conferences sponsored by non-profit and philanthropic organizations. His lectures address diverse audiences on a wide range of topics including religion, world politics, human relationships and societal evolution.

Over the span of more than 4 decades, Imam Faheem has dedicated his life to the upliftment of humanity. Along with other African American scholars (e.g., Asa Hilliard, Iyanla Van Zant, Dr. Na'im Akbar, et. al.), Imam Faheem Shuaibe has been inducted into the African American Intellectual Royal Family by the Institute for the Advance Study of Black Family Life and Culture. He is also a frequent lecturer at Cal Berkeley's "Holy Hill" for the Graduate Theological Union (GTU) which trains doctoral and post-doctoral students of Philosophy, and Theology.

To address issues he saw around the decline of marriage and family relationships, Imam Faheem founded M.A.R.I.A.M. (Muslim American Research Institute Advocating Marriage) which hosts regular conferences and discussions.

Mr. Shuaibe has also been recognized as a part of several distinguished delegations that have taken him around the globe on various educational, religious, interfaith, and peace missions including Saudi Arabia, Italy, Sudan, Malaysia, Egypt, The British Isles and the Caribbean. Passionate about interfaith relations, Imam Faheem is founding member of an "A list" of intellectuals, professionals, religious leaders and career diplomats on the "Abraham Family Reunion Project."

Imam Faheem is also the author of "The Reality of Our Sacred Human Nature: Our Origins and Our Destiny." You may find more of Imam Faheem's lectures and writings on one of his 6 weekly Blog Talk Radio shows under his *A Clear Understanding* Broadcasts: "Wealth Creation and Preservation," "All Things Human," "For those Who Thirst," "Universal Dimensions of Leadership," "The Qur'an Salat Institute," and "Juma'ah Live from Masjidul Waritheen in Oakland, California." His lectures are also broadcast on aclearunderstanding. net and are a rich source of inspiration and information to students across the country.

He has been married to Yolanda Mahasin Shuaibe for 46 years. They have 4 children and 3 grand-children.

You may reach him at sabilillah@aol.com.

Endnotes

1 12/28/1980 4th Sunday Hookup - Chicago, Ill

2 Randolph, Virginia, (1999)

3 Acknowledging and Distinguishing - hard/soft; rough/smooth; odor/fragrance; wet/dry; loud/quiet etc.

4 "Now, for all of these years that I have been working with the locks of secret knowledge nothing has been as rewarding to me as knowing that actually exactness in Scripture is abstract; and abstract in Scripture is exactness." Imam W. D. Mohammed (ra)

5 2: 60. And remember Moses prayed for water for his people; We said: "Strike the rock with thy staff." *[Use your capacity for logic]* Then gushed forth therefrom twelve springs *[Organized Universal Spiritual Nature; Natural Governance of Universal Spirituality]*. Each group *[Particularity]* knew its own place for water..." *(Spiritual Logic to build institutions to benefit society)*

6 *(See 6: 75-80; Star, Moon, Sun; Tauhid)* He represents the knowledge that preserves what is universal and in his universal composition it aids and helps and corrects that, that is local, and keeps it from going astray. So, he is really the universal teacher.

7 Abraham and the idols (21:57-66), Abraham versus Nimrod (2:258), Abraham and the Powers and the Laws of the Heavens and the Earth (6: 75-80), Abraham and the Sacrifice of his Son (37:102-106)

8 Another verse that speaks to the same feature of the Cosmos as a complement to the Human Nature is 65:12. "It is Allah who has created seven heavens and of the earth, the like of them. [His] command descends among them. So, you may know that Allah

is over all things competent and that Allah has encompassed all things in knowledge."

9   The numbering of this chapter and verse actually contains the origin and destiny of the original human potential 7 is the number of the potentialities that have to evolve up to 10 [Human conscience]. When this occurs, the person will have established their "true life" on earth. Until that happens it is an ongoing process of striving to unfold all (7) potentialities into the conscience (10).

10 Imam Warith Deen Muhammad "Imam's Retreat" Randolph, Virginia, January 16, 1999

11 P. 28 Wisdom of W. D. Mohammed, Part 2

12 Sura Tin ("Tin" is almost a homonym for the Quranic term translated as "clay") cannot be disconnected from this verse.

13 Sahih Bukhari Volume 001, Book 008, Hadith Number 345

14 There are different opinions regarding Adam as a Prophet or not. According to the hadeeth narrated by Ibn Hibbaan in his *Saheeh*, the Prophet (peace and blessings of Allah be upon him) was asked about Adam – was he a Prophet? He said, "Yes, a Prophet to whom Allah spoke." But he was not a Messenger, because of the hadeeth about intercession in which it says that the people will go to Nuh and say to him, "You are the first Messenger whom Allah sent to the earth." *Majmoo' Fataawa Ibn 'Uthaymeen*, 1/317

15 Imam W. D. Mohammed (RA) Imam's Retreat 1999 Randolph, Virginia

16 Imam Mohammed (RA) Ramadan Session October 23, 2005

17 https://tayyibaat.wordpress.com/2008/10/21/quranic-oath-by-the-fleeting-passage-of-time/
    Harf Qasm, a letter that shows there is an oath being taken. For example, we may say "wallahi", "by Allah!", which is: wa + Allah, the letter wow here is a harf qasm. Other letters in Arabic that signify that an oath is being taken are taa and laam.
    Maqsoom alayh, meaning the one whom (or that upon which)

the oath is being taken on. When we say "wallahi", we are swearing by Allah – so Allah is the maqsoom alayh.

Jawaab qasm, the response to [the reason for] the qasm. When someone swears, there is a reason for swearing, so "wallahi, I did this and that!" or "wallahi, I didn't lie!", so the *jawaab qasm* is, "I did this and that", or "I didn't lie."

The traditional opinion of qasm is that whatever Allah ta'ala swears by has been elevated and honored.

18 This phenomena of nature (masdar) connects with "Tie your camel and trust in Allah"(hadith) and with "I have created nothing more excellent and useful than you" (hadith) both of which connect to the importance of the faithful and obedient human intellect. The faithful and obedient human intellect rests upon the elaboration of the 5 senses. This masdari feature of the meaning also speaks to the intellect as a property not limited to males (See 33:35).

19 Sura Tin ("Tin" is almost a homonym for the quranic term translated as "clay") cannot be disconnected from this verse.

20 These two verses are numerical anagrams for each other. They both address the call for us to face of the forces and demands of nature.
    67:2. "He Who created Death and Life that He may try which of you is best in deed."

21 See 18:32 "The Parable Of The Man Who Was Given Two Gardens" and 34:15-16.
    55: 46. But for such as fear the time when they will stand before (the Judgment Seat of) their Lord there will be two Gardens
    47. Then which of the favors of your Lord will ye deny?

22 "The Biological Basis Of Thinking And Learning" Dr. Lawrence F. Lowery

23 Ramadan Session II, Masjid Taqwa, Saturday 7:00 am

24 Narrated by al-Bukhaari, 8; Muslim, 16.

25 Sahih Al-Bukhari 4:429

26 Imam W. D. Mohammed (RA) Imam's Retreat 1999 Randolph, Virginia

27 29: 19. See they not how Allah originates creation then repeats it: truly that is easy for Allah.

28 http://www.islamicbulletin.org/newsletters/issue_11/science.aspx

29 http://www.elnaggarzr.com/en/main.php?id=104

30 Malcolm X College Chicago, Ill. "Islam and Nationalism: How They Influence Each Other" 1/7-8/94

31 P. 22 Imam W. D. Mohammed (RA) "Thoughts for Searchers Published by Imam Ronald B. Shaheed

32 Kofsky, 1966; Allen, 1967; Lowery, 1981a.

33 36 Yahya is understood scripturally to be John, The Baptist, who purified people by ritually bathing them in a flowing river. By this we are connect to the Hadith of the Prophet(ﷺ) as well.

34 Sahih Al-Bukhari 4:429

35 Imam Mohammed (RA) was born in 1933.

36 Mary's "Moment", when she received the news of Jesus Christ, said, "O my Lord! How shall I have a son when no man hath touched me?" (3:47).

37 Metaphysically, this can be related to the "original human nature" being embedded in matter/the earth (as the womb of humanity) at the beginning of the human evolution and sojourn in the earth to Khalifah.

38 This further reinforces that, at this stage, "the life" is in a state of "undifferentiated duality."

39 http://www.elnaggarzr.com/en/main.php?id=104&Shift=1

40 This is not the publication for it but there is much food for thought in these verses and the story of how John, The Baptist

and Jesus Christ die in the Bible and what it means philosophi-
cally and metaphysically.

41 Sahih Al-Bukhari 4:429

42 Imam W. D. Mohammed (RA) Imam's Retreat 1999 Randolph,
Virginia

43 Important corollary between the story of Joseph
and Silver Production - https://www.youtube.com/
watch?v=h0n5NPMcd6U

44 There is at least a rhetorical connection to Jesus who spoke to
"The Woman at Jacob's Well that he gave to Joseph" about her 5
husbands. John 4: 1-26

45 This capability is "intuitive." It manifests in the child "without
formal instruction or being shown" Lowery p. 30

46 This is the name tradition gives to The Azziz's Wife.

47 This can also be related to "and the Jinn we created before…"

48 On the authority of Abu Muhammad Abdullah bin 'Amr bin
al-'Aas (RA) who said: The Messenger of Allah (SAW) said, "None
of you [truly] believes until his desires are subservient to that
which I have brought." [Imam an-Nawawi says:] We have related
it in Kitab al-Hujjah with a saheeh chain of narrators.

49 Abdullah b. Mas'ud reported that Allah's Messenger (may peace
be upon him) said: There is none amongst you with whom is not
attached to a jinn. The Companions said: Allah's Messenger, with
you too? Thereupon he said: Yes, but Allah helps me against him
and so I am safe from his hand and he does not command me but
for good." Sahih Muslim Book 39

50 I would (not) be surprised at all, if this word is not the Arabic
word from which English took "grass."

51 The palindrome, [reading the same backwards and forward],
insight in the numbering of this verse (71:17) actually contains
the entire message of the sacred life movement from concrete
to abstract. From 7 physical stages in the womb to evolve 1 body

with a brain and then that 1 brain evolves 7 stages to achieve its full capability in the world.

52 http://www.aol.com/article/2016/02/02/kid-has-a-brutally-honest-answer-to-a-ridiculous-assignment/21306859/

53 Dr. Lawrence Lowery "Thinking and Learning: Matching Developmental Stage with Curriculum"

54 Sahih Al-Bukhari 4:429

55 Imam W. D. Mohammed (RA) Imam's Retreat 1999 Randolph, Virginia

56 Imam Mohammed, Ash shams: Enlightenment of the Soul, Little Rock, Arkansas,

57 [p. 784 Kitab Al-Ain]

58 http://www.islamicbulletin.org/newsletters/issue_11/science.aspx

59 Teeth are a part of the skeletal system but they are not considered "bone." https://www.livescience.com/33130-why-are-teeth-not-considered-bones.html

60 The average "4th" grader is 9 or 10 years old.

61 Dr. Lawrence Lowery "Thinking and Learning: Matching Developmental Stage With Curriculum"

62 This is also the "end point" of the hadith regarding Nutfah (40 days), Alaqa (40 days) and Mudghata (40 days) then the Angel comes and writes.... Bukhari Vol. 4 Book 55 No. 549

63 In current teaching methodology there is a process called "Chunk, Chew and Check" Video - https://www.youtube.com/watch?v=pkbSfGHoKbk. The method says that "Chewing is where the learning takes place."

64 See Imam Mohammed's "The Growth Of Human Consciousness."

65 The establishment of the speech ability and the Hyoid Bone.

66 39:18 Those who listen to the Word, and follow the best (meaning) in it: those are the ones whom Allah has guided, and those are the ones endued with understanding.

67 Imam W. D. Mohammed (RA) Imam's Retreat 1999 Randolph, Virginia

68 Omar Dictionary, p. 590. You know that language has those subtle hints and Allah said they believe that man was made from clay and Allah said "from sounding clay", potters' clay that makes a sound. It rings. So the wisdom there, the Guidance there, I understand it to be, is that man has to have an ear for the sound of words. How they sound. Ash shams: Enlightenment of the Soul Little Rock, Arkansas

69 This is another instance which demonstrates that having the insights for reading the Quran that Imam Mohammed is valuable for guidance. "You can't touch me"; "You can't move me. Because I have no sympathy for you" I'm only interested in my own desires." It means you will be deprived of human sensitivities and the masses of society will dislike you. And because of your greed all of your wealth will drive you insane in this world and you will burn in hell after this life. (Ayn Rand – Objectivism; Scrooge, Madoff, "Wolf of Wall Street," etc.)

70 12-28-80 Imam Warith Deen Muhammed National Broadcast

71 This understanding can be read from Sura 2:143-151. The change of the Qibla from Jerusalem to Mecca was a type of correction. The Old Qibla [Jerusalem] was for some a "Golden Calf/Sacred Cow" which some were unwilling to give up. The Old Qibla had its past excellence [like the jewels and precious metals used to make the Golden Calf] but the problem of the Old Qibla was that its foundation was particular not universal. The invitation in this set of verses is for each one to find their particularly excellence and put it to use in their particular place [e.g., culture; community] but in the interest of the universal destiny of humanity – The Sacred House.

72 Sahih Al-Bukhari 4:429

73 Bones: Level V

74 HQ 23:14

75 Imam W. D. Mohammed (RA) Imam's Retreat 1999 Randolph, Virginia

76 See the supplementary commentary on HQ 2:16-20

77 Scientific American Mind August/September 2008

78 See "Soundness and Validity" in Supplementary section

79 Simply put what Moses did was not magic just as what the Qur'an is is not Poetry.

80 This understanding can be read from Sura 2:143-151. The change of the Qibla from Jerusalem to Mecca was a type of correction. The Old Qibla [Jerusalem] was for some a "Golden Calf/Sacred Cow" which some were unwilling to give up. The Old Qibla had its past excellence [like the jewels and precious metals used to make the Golden Calf] but the problem of the Old Qibla was that its foundation was particular not universal. The invitation in this set of verses is for each one to find their particularly excellence and put it to use in their particular place [e.g., culture; community] but in the interest of the universal destiny of humanity – The Sacred House.

81 Sahih Al-Bukhari 4:429; Abbas Ibn Malik reported that Malik Ibn Sasaa said that Allah's Messenger described to them his Night Journey.

82 This was done in the Level V state "Aaron/Haroun." The leadership was "bones without flesh." Following a logic without human sensitivity.

83 Imam W. D. Mohammed (RA) Imam's Retreat 1999 Randolph, Virginia

84 P. 79 "Education A Sacred Matter" Imam W. D. Mohammed (RA) published by Imam Ronald B. Shaheed

85 P. 38 "The Promised Human Destiny" Imam W. D. Mohammed (RA) published by Imam Ronald B. Shaheed.

86 Sahih Muslim, Book 030

87 Miskat Al Masabih

88 9-1-96 "Al-Islam the Force And The Rise of Our Community, the Light Is On" Convention White Plains N.Y.

89 "Education: A Sacred Matter" Page 119

90 Dr. Lawrence Lowery "Thinking and Learning: Matching Developmental Stage With Curriculum"

91 One of the reasons the term "theory" is used is because it acknowledges that only G-d ["Theo"] knows the reality. It reminds the scientific community that what we seem to be certain about so far ["Our Theory"] regarding "this or that" phenomena in nature is still "subject to change."

92 This final stage in scientific history is dawning in our time. Alhamdulillah!

93 We believe that every part of "The Kitab" is part of the revelation. This verse's numbering is 3:97. Consequently, intuition leads us to search for "3" in the 97th Sura. We find that "Lailatul Qadr" is mentioned 3 times in that Sura. This further leads intuition to look back into the Qur'an [Al-Kitab] which states that man's evolution is out of "3 Veils of Darkness" [39:6]. Even the numbering of that verses solves to "9" which is the "fullness of 3." Furthermore, remove the colon from the verse annotations and you get 396 and 397 to leave no doubt, "for those who believe", that the verses are "closely connected." These connections point to the Tauhid of creation and of human nature, which was Abraham's ultimate discovery and he memorialized with the building of the Ka'aba.

94 Sahih al-Bukhari 3355

95 Luke 20:17

96 (Bukhari)

97 Mohammed is the realization of Adam to Abraham in actuality.

98 "Education: A Sacred Matter" P. 131

99 Matthew 21:42; Luke 20:17

100 Proverbs 23:7

101 https://www.al-islam.org/islamic-stories/
here-comes-al-amin-trustworthy

102 HQ 20:115

103 HQ 2:37

104 This is one of the conclusive meanings from HQ 4:28 "Khuliqal
Insaanu Da-eefan" when the grammar is understood.

105 HQ 17:70

106 See the Supplement for the Imam's Teaching on "The Sabbath
Breakers."

107 The Imam is also speaking from 7:157 "...and follow the light
that was sent down with him"

108 See Surah 60:4,6; 33:21

109 HQ 20:14

110 **Gen 17:3**; Abraham prostrated ; **Matt. 26:39**; Jesus prostrated

Made in the USA
San Bernardino, CA
13 August 2020

77016106R00078